BLACK ROBE PEACEMAKER

Pierre De Smet

BLACK ROBE PEACEMAKER

Pierre De Smet

By
J. G. E. Hopkins

Illustrated by W. N. Wilson

HILLSIDE EDUCATION

Cover and interior book design by Mary Jo Loboda

Front Cover: "Missionaries arrive at Fort Hall on August 15, 1841" by
Fr. Nicholas Point, From *Wilderness Kingdom, The Journals and Paintings of Fr. Jerome Point* by Loyola University Press, Chicago, 1967.

Back Cover: Moses Linton , "A Drawing of the St. Mary's Mission in
1841 from the Moses Linton Album," *Crossings and Dwellings: Restored
Jesuits, Women Religious, American Experience 1814-2014*, accessed
March 22, 2019, http://students.ctsdh.luc.edu/projects/omeka/kyle2/
items/show/279, and *Crow Indian Chief Big Shadow (Big Robber)*
painted by Father De Smet, courtesy of Wikimedia.

ISBN: 978-0-9991706-7-0

Hillside Education
475 Bidwell Hill Road
Lake Ariel, PA 18436
www.hillsideeducation.com

CONTENTS

BLACK ROBE PEACEMAKER

Pierre De Smet

Chapter 1

FROM THE OLD WORLD TO THE NEW

Early one springtime morning in the year 1812, the good people of Termonde—a Belgian town about twenty-five miles southwest of the great port of Antwerp—woke up to a noise of cheering and shouting. A crowd of schoolboys had gathered in one of the town squares, and a stocky, blue-eyed, broad-shouldered lad was making them a speech.

"We'll take the town before they know we're there," he cried. "They won't have guards out this early in the morning. On to victory!"

"Hooray," the boys shouted. "Hooray for General Samson!"

For weeks this exciting game of war had been going on. The boys of Grembergen, a neighboring village, were the Russian and Austrian enemy; the Termonde boys (in their imaginations, at least) were the invincible grenadiers of the Emperor Napoleon.

Older and wiser people might hate Napoleon Bonaparte for the bloodshed and ruin he had brought on Europe, but Belgian boys felt that they shared somehow in the military glory of his victories. They had listened to the stories told by fellow townsmen who'd followed the imperial eagles through Italy and Spain and Germany, and they longed for the day when they'd be grown up and could put on a uniform.

With whoops and shouts they followed "General Samson" headlong down the Grembergen road. Just as they reached a line of hills outside that village, the "Russians and Austrians" fell on them from ambush. Spies had been at work. The surprise attack was no surprise. For a minute or two the battle was even. Fists and sticks were busily at work. Then the Grembergen boys broke and ran up the winding main street to the church square. "Samson" and his men pursued them with cries of victory, but not for long.

It was a Sunday morning, and out of the church poured the fathers, uncles and big brothers of the defeated force. They didn't stop to ask questions. With clubs and pitchfork handles they beat such a tattoo on the heads and shoulders of "Samson's" army that it turned tail and ran.

The sting of defeat and a large lump on his head weren't all that poor "Samson" had to suffer. As he and his troops entered Termonde on the double, the first man he met was a very angry father; for the next ten days he was forbidden to leave the house.

"Samson's" real name was Pierre Jean De Smet. At the time of the great battle of Grembergen he was eleven years old, the strongest and most daring boy of his age in Termonde. No one could beat him at wrestling or foot racing. He loved to climb tall trees and swing himself down from limb to limb; he was a leader in the dangerous game of leaping from boat to boat in motion on the nearby rivers Dender and Scheldt.

"God keep him!" his father used to say when Pierre Jean repeated long tales of adventure from the books he was always reading. "He'll never stay at home. He'll be either a soldier or a wanderer."

And his brother Charles, who was three years older and as sensible and careful as Pierre was heedless and wild, had his hands full keeping the little brother in line.

The father was named Joost De Smet. He was a boatbuilder and well-to-do, a stern man but a fair one. He and his wife, Marie Jeanne Buydens De Smet, had bred the virtues of piety and hard work into their many children from the cradle. Such solid families were the rule in Flanders, as the part of Belgium where they lived was called.

For centuries the nations of Europe had used Flanders as a battlefield for their many wars; but after each conflict the Flemish people had gone to work to restore all that had been looted or destroyed. Patience and thoroughness were parts of a Flemish boy's inheritance. All during Pierre Jean's childhood Napoleon Bonaparte had been master of Belgium, but by the time the boy was ready to go away to boarding school, the battle of Waterloo had been fought, and the fallen emperor was a prisoner on the far-off island of St. Helena.

Pierre's teachers didn't consider him very bright. He was fond of reading, and he liked to write little essays, but whatever honors he won in school were won on the playing field. There, he was first in everything. He could hold his arms straight out, tense his muscles, and defy any four of his schoolmates to bend the arms down. He seemed unaware of fear. Yet he never bullied anyone or abused his great strength, and the teachers and schoolboys all liked him for his kindness, his cheerfulness, and for his plain common sense.

At the college of Alost, which Pierre entered in 1818, it was the same story. He held his own in studies but excelled in all sports. He never seemed to care what he would do in life, however, and his father was beginning to wonder if this strong, smiling, easygoing dreamer would ever amount to anything. Business didn't interest him, or any of the professions, and, when he left Alost to enter the preparatory seminary at Mechlin, he was not even sure he wanted to be a priest.

Although not outwardly "pious" he was a good young man and felt drawn to the service of God. Still, he could not be sure where he might best serve Him. Joost De Smet would shake his head when some of this uncertainty appeared in the letters that Pierre wrote home from the seminary.

In 1821 a stranger came to stay a few days at the seminary— Father Charles Nerinckx, an adventurous Belgian who had gone as a missionary to the United States in 1804. He and another priest had all Kentucky for their parish. Now he'd come back to his native land to beg for money to build churches and mission stations. He was recruiting young men for the Society of Jesus, the Jesuits, who desperately needed priests in the United States.

The seminarians crowded into the lecture hall to hear Father Nerinckx tell of his long journeys in the heat of summer and the winter cold, fording rivers on horseback or swimming them when necessary, to serve a parish larger than all France. Thousands of Catholics in the older states were losing their religion, he said, because there were so few priests to hearten and instruct them. Out on the frontier, the settlers wondered and thanked God whenever a priest rode up to their cabins in the forest clearings. And beyond the frontier were thousands upon thousands of Indians—whole tribes and nations—who were ignorant not only of God but of everything that might raise them out of savagery.

"Napoleon found millions of men ready to sacrifice their lives to ravage nations and destroy them," Father Nerinckx concluded sadly. "I cannot find even a handful of men eager to save entire peoples and extend the reign of God."

Many of the young men who sat listening were deeply moved by the missionary's words, but Pierre Jean De Smet felt that they had been spoken directly to him. He had always liked to read travelers' tales about the gloomy forests and broad rivers of the American West, and he had dreamed of seeing them someday. Now Father Nerinckx was giving him a noble purpose for his dreaming.

His quick imagination called up images of dark faces streaked with war paint, of savage hunters in wild pursuit of buffalo over the vast plains. All along he had felt that his life was not meant to be lived in placid Belgium, but where and how his strength of body and love of adventure might serve some worthwhile end had never before occurred to him.

There was no doubt about it, he thought, as he sat in his room searching his soul—God was calling him to preach the Gospel in America, to work among the Indians, to be a Jesuit. He had studied the history of the Jesuits; they were men after his own heart. Peter Canisius had won half of Germany back from Lutheranism. Edmund Campion had confounded the wise men at Elizabeth of England's court, even as he stood in the shadow of the headsman's axe.

In the New World, Isaac Jogues and Jacques Marquette had broken trails through the very wilderness where he could see himself ranging. Like them, he would make it his business to study and understand the strange and savage red men—and to love them because they also were children of God.

Many of the seminarians at Mechlin went to Father Nerinckx and offered to go with him to America. Only nine were accepted.

Pierre De Smet was one of them.

But there were difficulties in his way. The Dutch government wouldn't allow any Catholic missionary to leave the country if it knew the purpose of his journey. The nine seminarians would have to make their way secretly to Amsterdam and conceal themselves there until their ship was ready to sail.

Pierre had no money, but that problem was solved by the sale of some of his books and clothes, and by gifts from charitable folk who wanted to help him. The chief difficulty lay inside himself. How was he going to break the news to his father? Joost De Smet was certain to look on his son's decision as just one more example of heedlessness—another rash act of a headstrong boy. There might be hours, even days, of wrangling if he went home and told his family what he intended to do. And since he meant to go anyway, what was the point in wasting words?

In the end, he decided not to visit Termonde. Once his ship was beyond recall, he would send a letter of farewell and explanation back with the pilot. Many of his friends might consider him heartless, but he preferred to remember his family as he had known them, rather than go from them in bitterness.

The last week of July 1821 was hot and sultry. As he waited in the garret room where all the young missionaries lay hiding until the time of their departure, Pierre Jean's spirits sank lower and lower. It was bad enough having to skulk like a criminal here in Amsterdam; it was worse not to be able to get his family off his mind. Surely they had discovered his absence by now, and who could tell what meaning they might give to it? How hurt and puzzled they must be!

At times he was tempted to risk everything and send his father the long letter he had prepared. Yet if he did so, his father would find some way of detaining him. It was too much to hope that the old man would keep his temper long enough to study all the good reasons which the letter gave for his son's action.

Pierre Jean tried to read, but he couldn't fix his attention on a book. In the little room where the young men huddled the air was stifling. He felt he must get out and walk, even if the police should collar him. But surely the police of a great city had more to do than prowl about with eyes peeled for one young nobody from the country.

Out on the street, moving among strangers, he felt better. He strode along vigorously, looking eagerly at all the unfamiliar sights. So interested was he in what lay before him that he never noticed a man who came thrusting through the crowd. Just as he was crossing one of the bridges that span the canals of Amsterdam, he was seized by the arm and spun roughly around. There, red in the face with the heat and his exertions, was his brother Charles.

"A fine thing!" began Charles. "I've been looking everywhere for you. You must come home at once."

"I'm sorry," Pierre Jean replied calmly. "I can't. I've made an engagement, and I must keep it."

"You've made a fool of yourself, you mean." Charles's raised voice caused people to stop and stare at the two sturdy young men. "Your engagement, as you call it, is the talk of Flanders."

"All the more reason why it shouldn't be the talk of Amsterdam," answered Pierre Jean with a smile. "Let's go to my room, if you must argue with me."

The presence of the other young men in the room didn't embarrass Charles at all. He paced up and down, scolding his brother, while Pierre Jean sat and listened quietly.

"Our father's more than eighty—he's too good a man to be treated this way. Why didn't you let us know what you were going to do? Why did we have to learn about it from strangers—from gossip? We were half sick with worry." He paused a moment, and then continued: "What ever made you do it? Had you any reason at all?"

"They need priests in America."

"Europe needs priests, too." Charles waved his hand impatiently. "Do you have to travel across the ocean to become one, and break our father's heart? Be reasonable, brother. Go back to the seminary and be ordained. Stay in Belgium and serve those who love you and need you.

Nothing would please Father more, or me, or any of us. Then perhaps, when Father is dead and when you're sure you know your own mind, you can go adventuring on the foreign missions."

"This is no adventure, Charles." Pierre Jean got up and went to one of the little dormer windows ; he stood looking out over the rooftops of the city. "I'm not amusing myself. I want to serve God. Oh, I know that you and Father think I'm still a wild boy, who must be guided and kept from doing himself harm. That was true once, but not any more. Day and night, these past two years, I've thought about myself and what I must do. I prayed hard for guidance. Sometimes I wondered if my vocation was to be a monk, a Trappist even. I studied the rules and the history of all the Orders and Congregations, and still I couldn't see where I'd fit in. That day when Father Nerinckx told us about America, it was just as if he'd opened a door and shown me what I'd been looking for all those weary months. I was called to be a Jesuit, and in America. I was as sure of it as you're sure you want to be a lawyer."

He turned about, his blue eyes bright and merry and confident. "I'm sorry I've given you so much trouble. I should have told our Father—it would have been kinder; but you must realize that I've made up my mind. I know I'll never be learned or very wise, but I'm strong, and too foolish to be afraid of anything. Isn't that what they need on the American missions?"

"I do believe you mean what you say," replied Charles, after a long silence. "If Father could hear you, he might believe it, too. But you never gave us any idea—we thought you were wasting your time."

"I was, but I shan't waste any more."

"Very well, then." Completely convinced, in an instant Charles became the brisk man of business. Now he was as eagerly on his brother's side as he had been against him.

"I'll make your peace with Father," he promised. "Be sure to write him, though, and make him see your reasons the way you've made me see them. Won't you need money? Here, take this." He pulled out his purse and pressed a handful of banknotes on Pierre Jean. "No, don't thank me. Now that I'm satisfied you know what you're doing, I wish it were twice as much. If you need more when you get to America, write me for it."

A few days later the young missionaries left Amsterdam to go aboard the American brig *Columbia* at the Texel; on the feast of the Assumption they cleared for Philadelphia.

For eighteen months after their arrival in their new country Pierre Jean and his companions studied, mastered their wills, and sought "virtue, duty, and God alone," according to the rules laid down for the Jesuit novitiate. Father Anthony Kohlmann, the Provincial of the Jesuits in the eastern United States, had been happy to receive so promising a group of young volunteers. He had sent them to receive their training at Whitemarsh, a plantation some twenty-five miles from the city of Washington.

There they were to work and study under the eye of Father Charles Van Quickenborne, the novice master; a Belgian like themselves, he was a stern, self-denying and heroic man. In addition to his regular work, he served two parishes as pastor, held instruction classes for the Negroes in the neighborhood, and was carpenter, architect, stonemason and farmer as occasion required these skills.

My father and Charles should see me now, thought Pierre Jean as he drove a plow over the fields of the Whitemarsh farm or swung an ax in the woodlot. There wasn't anything the least bit romantic about his life in the novitiate; now that he'd seen America and knew how vast it was, he had to smile at his first notions of what it meant to be a missionary there.

Here in rural Maryland, the Indians of the wild West seemed even farther away than they'd seemed in Belgium. The impulse to win those tawny nations to God was still strong in Pierre Jean, but he was perfectly resigned to work wherever he was needed. Perhaps it would be God's will that he'd never see an Indian—that he'd never go West. If so, he'd be content. For never in his life had he felt so happy, so at peace with himself.

Then at the beginning of the year 1823 came startling and wonderful news. Bishop William Dubourg of New Orleans asked the Jesuit Provincial to start a mission to the Indian tribes west of the Mississippi and along the Missouri. He offered the missionaries a large farm for their support; it lay near Florissant, a village about sixteen miles from the city of St. Louis. Father Van Quickenborne was appointed Superior of the new mission and Pierre Jean was one of ten others selected to go because of their fitness for the task.

"I thank God I am one of those chosen," he wrote to his family. "Pray for me and my companions."

There was no money for traveling expenses, so the little company loaded their baggage on two wagons and started off for Missouri on foot. On their way they cooked their own meals; each night they found shelter in barns or abandoned cabins. After eighteen days of tramping they arrived at Wheeling on the Ohio River. Here they bought two scows and lashed them together to make a raft. On this makeshift craft they floated down the river past the dense forests that lined its course, past clusters of cabins, past little towns that are now great cities like Cincinnati and Louisville, until they came to Shawneetown—a settlement which lay a short distance above the junction of the Ohio with the Mississippi River.

Although the voyage down the Ohio was dangerous and difficult, Father Van Quickenborne never let the laboring novices forget that they were Jesuits in training. Each morning Mass was said. And despite sudden windstorms and the menace of snags in the water, the times for prayer, for meditation, and for examination of conscience were strictly kept. As for Pierre Jean, the thought that each mile was bringing him closer to the Indian country made all his labors light.

They abandoned the raft at Shawneetown, for it wouldn't be possible to take it upriver against the swift current of the Mississippi. They sent their baggage on to St. Louis by steamboat and set off on foot across the marshes of southern Illinois—a journey of almost two hundred miles over prairie drowned by the spring rains, often in water up to their waists. Day and night, clouds of mosquitoes sang about their ears.

On May 31 they came in sight of St. Louis, in those days a booming town of about five thousand people. River craft of every size and shape were tied up to the levee. In the streets, bewhiskered fur trappers, fresh from the mountains, rubbed shoulders with broad-clothed emigrants from the East. The shops and trading sheds were loud with laughter and the hearty give-and-take of shrewd bargainers. Pierre's spirits rose as he looked around him. This was what he'd dreamed of; here was where he belonged.

Chapter 2

WHITE MEN AND RED

Florissant was a lovely spot, green and fertile and bounded by forests of oak, walnut and maple, but the first years which Pierre Jean and his companions spent there were years of grinding poverty and hardship. The new mission was so poor that often the men didn't have enough to eat. The Bishop had no money to give them. They had to depend entirely on themselves. They cleared their land, built log huts for shelter, and worked long hours in the fields while they continued their studies in philosophy and theology. But Pierre Jean took it all in stride. "Back home," he wrote his father, "I often had to be bled, which required a doctor. Here, it's done free— by gnats, fleas, ticks, flies and mosquitoes."

In spite of all the difficulties, the tireless Father Van Quickenborne and a single assistant professor saw to it that the men in their charge received a thorough grounding in their studies. On September 23, 1827, Pierre Jean and three of his fellow scholastics were ordained to the priesthood. But his dream of going among the Indian tribes still seemed as far off as ever.

The situation around St. Louis, and in Missouri generally, had altered so in four years that the Jesuits had changed their plans. There was more than enough work for them to do among the settlers who had come thronging in to Missouri, so the Jesuits couldn't spare a single priest for a mission in

Indian country. The unhappy tribes along the lower Missouri River had been driven westward from their homes in Indiana, Michigan, Illinois and Wisconsin and settled at random by the government on land which didn't suit them. They had sent messengers to the pastor of the St. Louis Cathedral to ask for Black Robes, as they called priests, but the best that could be done for them was the erection of a boarding school for their children at Florissant.

Father De Smet—as we shall call him now—took a great interest in this school. Children from eight different tribes came there, and while the young priest taught them to read and write and tried to interest them in farming, he did his best to master their languages and understand their ways of thinking. It was a beginning at least of what he wanted so much to do.

Meanwhile, the city of St. Louis was growing so fast, and the need for a school and college there under Catholic guidance had become so apparent, that the Jesuits opened one in the fall of 1829. It is today the great St. Louis University. Many students, both Catholic and Protestant, flocked to it, and the few Jesuits available to serve on its faculty were badly overworked. Father De Smet gave up his tasks at the Indian school to be dean and professor of English at the new college. He was also appointed its procurator, or treasurer, for he had shown a surprising talent for business. A shrewd businessman was needed, for pennies had to be counted and much money raised to pay for the new college buildings and to support the novices at Florissant. Begging, bargaining and haggling were not to Father De Smet's taste, but he went cheerfully about his work. "I am Father Procurator," he wrote to one of his sisters, "I, who could never keep a penny in my pocket."

The efforts of Father De Smet and the charity of the Missouri Catholics were not enough. The college and the novitiate had to have more money. In the summer of 1833 the Jesuits decided that someone must go to Belgium and beg for help. As even his iron physique had begun to show signs of wear under the strain of his duties, they felt that Father De Smet should be the man. He could appeal to the charity of their countrymen and enjoy a well-earned holiday at the same time.

Cheerful and obedient as always, he left St. Louis in September and landed in France at Le Havre shortly after the new year, 1834. His family and his old friends were delighted to see him, but he couldn't stay more than a few days at Termonde. He then set off on a backbreaking tour of all the Belgian towns and cities, begging for money, for books and laboratory apparatus, and especially for young men to join the Jesuit missionaries in America. He met with success, but in early November, just at the start of his voyage back to America, his years of overwork took their toll. He fell desperately sick. The captain of the ship on which he'd embarked turned back and set him ashore in England. After several weeks he was well enough to make his way home to Termonde, but the doctors told him that months—perhaps years—must pass before he could think of returning to St. Louis.

At first Father De Smet was utterly discouraged. Here he lay stricken and useless, yet he'd hardly begun the work to which he had dedicated himself. He tried to comfort himself with the thought that God has His designs in all that happens. And he made up his mind to a sacrifice that, to him, would be the greatest of all sacrifices. Rather than put the Society of Jesus to the expense of maintaining a man who could do nothing, he would resign from it. This he did on May 8, 1835.

For two years he lived at home in Termonde. He could have been accepted as a secular priest at Ghent, but he chose to do what little he could in his own town. He served as business agent for the local orphanage, and was spiritual director of the convent of Carmelites. The missionaries in St. Louis didn't forget him; they wrote often to him, hoping that God would give him the strength to return to them someday. Nor did he neglect them. He helped organize a society to raise money for their work, and he never ceased urging the superiors of seminaries in Belgium and Holland to encourage vocations to the American missions.

Little by little Father De Smet began to feel better. When he walked now, it was with the old, free stride; when he worked, it was with his one-time vigor and joy in getting something done. As his health improved he began to doubt the wisdom of his resignation from the Jesuits. While he lay at death's door, it had seemed like an act of generosity; now that he was almost himself again, it seemed more like an act of weakness. No one had asked him to resign. Could it have been pride that had made him do it? Whatever the reason, it had been a mistake and he meant to correct it as soon as he could. Four missionaries were leaving for St. Louis in September 1837, and despite a relapse that almost upset his plan, Father De Smet accompanied them. On the twenty-ninth of November he reached St. Louis in good health, and Father Peter Verhaegen, the Superior of the mission, received him back into his beloved Society.

The city of St. Louis had grown and prospered during his absence. The college was firmly on its feet, and the Jesuits could now turn to the task for which they'd come to Missouri fourteen years before—the conversion of the western Indian tribes. Father Van Quickenborne, who had retired as Superior to give all his time to the establishment of Indian missions in Missouri, had already made a start among the Osages, Iowas and Kickapoos. The Indians, resentful of the treatment they had received from the government of the United States, soon turned to thieving and liquor and cared little for anything the missionaries had to say. Up the Missouri River, however, at Council Bluffs, the Potawatomis had been settled. They had come recently from their home in Michigan and their chiefs had asked that a Black Robe be sent to live with them.

Father De Smet begged his superiors to give him the assignment. He prayed for it, and he asked his friends to pray that he'd get it. "I tremble when I think what great qualities an apostolate to the Indians demands," he wrote to his friends, the Carmelite Sisters at Termonde. "We must make men out of them before making Christians, and such work requires unlimited patience and solid virtue."

This was only too true, as he soon found. On May 10, 1838, having received the appointment to the Potawatomi mission, he set off up the Missouri River. At Leavenworth, Father Felix Verreydt and Brother Mazelli, two other Jesuits, joined him. The boat was heavily loaded, and in order to buck the swift current, the engineer kept the steam at full pressure so that the boilers groaned and wheezed. Sand bars tried the pilot's skill, and snags—the upthrust roots of submerged trees carried down by the spring floods. A snag could rip the bottom out of any boat.

"I would rather cross the ocean," he wrote, "than ascend the Missouri River." After a difficult journey of three weeks they came to Council Bluffs. Almost two thousand Indians, painted and carrying arms, thronged to the landing to stare at the Black Robes, but the four or five hundred fervent Catholics of whom they had been told at St. Louis were nowhere to be seen. Only the half-breed chief, William Caldwell, and a couple of Indian families made them welcome.

The village itself was a desolate place, a helter-skelter assembly of *tipis* (tents) covered with bark, buffalo skins or canvas. The women did all the rough work of the camp; the men sat idle all day, playing cards and smoking their pipes. To work was beneath their dignity. Their only possessions were a few horses, turned out to graze. They took no interest at all in Father De Smet or his mission.

He was too vigorous a man to be easily discouraged, nor were his companions willing to give up. They shared the rough life of the Indians and did their best to help them. Father De Smet and Brother Mazelli spent much time with the sick, going from village to village with their simple medicines and coping with the frequent epidemics which the filth and shiftlessness of the Indians brought on.

"My shelter is a hut fourteen feet square," Father De Smet wrote his brother. "It is made of trunks of fallen trees and roofed with rough shingles. My furniture is a crucifix, a small table, a bench and a pile of books. A piece of meat and some wild roots, washed down with spring water, is about my only food. My gun is my constant companion. Bears and starved wolves prowl about here. And there is a war going on between the Indians. Bands of Otoes, Pawnees and Sioux are roaming in every direction, seeking scalps."

As soon as the Indians saw that the Black Robes wanted nothing for themselves, their suspicions melted away. Father De Smet's fearless and kindly manner impressed them, and many Potawatomis asked to be instructed in the Faith. The little wooden church of St. Joseph began to fill up and in the first year of the mission more than three hundred of the tribe were baptized. When the neighboring Omahas and Loup Pawnees began to show signs of interest the missionaries were happier still.

One fact forced itself on Father De Smet's mind during his first year among the western Indians. The attempt which the government was making to "civilize" them all at once was futile. Anyone could see that it would be years before Indians could live like white men. It must be a slow process, and it would succeed only if the white man's good example convinced the Indians that "civilization" was worth having.

Many years before, in South America, the Jesuits had worked successfully among the tribes of Paraguay. Before the greed and treachery of European politicians ruined it all, the Jesuits had made the natives self-reliant and had taught them to be proud of their accomplishments. Their grandchildren had become skilled craftsmen, farmers, even artists. Was such a work impossible in North America? Father De Smet

didn't think so.

First things had to come first, however. If the arts of peace were to be taught, peace must be secured, and the settling of the Potawatomis on lands which the great Sioux nation considered their property had brought on something close to war. The Yankton and Santee branches of the Sioux were already raiding the outlying Potawatomi villages.

In the spring of 1839 Father De Smet set out on the first of his many successful peace missions. He had no clever scheme in mind; no powerful force to back up his words. He intended merely to visit the Sioux chiefs in their camp at the mouth of the Vermillion River and explain to them that the Potawatomis had not moved to the Missouri country by their own choice. He was confident that even savage peoples would act generously, once they knew the facts.

Whether because the Sioux admired his complete fearlessness in coming to them, or because they were impressed by that quality of goodness and honesty which everyone who met him sensed in him, they received him kindly and listened to what he had to say. At the end of the talk, the Sioux chiefs agreed to let the Potawatomis alone. More than that, they sent presents to the families of those Potawatomis who had lost their lives in the raids. By Indian custom, no peace was considered settled until the dead were "covered" in this fashion. And when Father De Smet took advantage of the occasion to speak to them about religion, several Sioux asked for baptism—the start of a missionary work among that nation which was later to be of great importance.

All seemed well when he returned to the Potawatomi villages, but now he was about to see for the first time the white man's disregard of the promises made to the Indians.

On August 19 the Potawatomi men, women and children came crowding in from the villages to the government agency for the annual distribution of money. The government had promised them $50,000 yearly in return for their surrender of their lands in Michigan. The money was supposed to be spent for food and on the improvement of their new homes.

Early that morning Father De Smet went down to the landing. The steamer *Antelope* was due, bringing provisions and mail from St. Louis, but the priest was not so much concerned with that as with his fears for what the day would bring forth. The news that the Indians would have a great sum of money to spend had already brought up some shady white men from the settlements—cheating peddlers, cardsharps anxious to take advantage of the Indians' love of gambling, and shabby scoundrels of every description.

The *Antelope* sounded her deep-toned whistle as she came in sight. The waiting crowd cheered. She swung slowly round, her paddle wheel churning up the muddy water, and then drove hard against the current until her nose touched the bank. Her deck hands threw out lines and they were quickly made fast to the landing.

The passengers scurried down the gangplank, eager to land or to stretch their legs for a while before they continued the voyage upriver. There were trappers bound for Fort Union and the fur country, an army officer or two, and many regular Indian traders whose faces were familiar; but there were many others, newcomers, whose hard faces made the priest think that his fears were going to be justified only too soon. A voice called to him from the pilothouse, and Father De Smet looked up to see the pleasant smile and waving hand of his friend Captain La Barge—Joe La Barge as everyone called him—the finest young pilot on the Missouri.

A bugle sounded from the agency buildings; the distribution of money was about to begin. Most of the crowd hurried away to be present at the ceremony, but the priest was more interested in what was going on at the *Antelope's* after-cargo port. Some men had brought out long wooden skids or runners and were setting them up near the landing stage. Others were sweating and cursing as they set their shoulders to a huge cask, preparing to roll it up to the skids. In spite of the laws against selling whisky or brandy to the Indians, here were a set of ruffians preparing to do so.

Father De Smet's face flamed with anger. All his self-control and customary gentleness flew from him as he thought what would happen to the mission if the whisky sellers were allowed to have their way. Some woodsman had left a broad-bladed ax leaning against the wall of a building nearby. Father De Smet seized it and ran at top speed down to the place where the cask was being set up. He thrust three men reeling out of his way with one sweep of his arm, swung the ax high in the air, and brought it down on the cask with all his strength. The wood seemed to burst apart. The rotgut which the cask contained spilled out on the ground.

A yell of anger rose from the men, and from their mates aboard the *Antelope* who were getting ready to land a second cask. One of the men he had felled came sliding like a snake along the ground and slashed at him with a long knife. He fell back a little, swinging the ax before him to keep the rest of the bewhiskered, evil-looking crowd at bay. But he had put himself in a bad position. Behind him, a clay bank rose abruptly and cut off any farther retreat; the dozen or more whisky sellers had fanned out and were coming at him from three sides. He was trapped. And in this wild country it was

kill or be killed.

His friends from the landing who might have rallied to help him had all gone up to the agency; only the scum of the settlement were left, and they did nothing but stand and stare and yell. Then, just as the whisky sellers were about to rush him and make an end of him, a man dropped down beside him from the top of the bank—a tall, lean, broad-shouldered man in a frock coat. He held a pistol in each hand.

"That'll do now," said Captain La Barge, for it was he. "I've two lives here in my guns—and my friend's handy with an ax, as you've had a chance to see."

"He busted in our keg," cried the leader of the whisky sellers fiercely. "We're a-goin' to cut him fer it. Yaas, and you, too, if ye're not keerful."

"I don't think so," the captain replied in a deceptively mild voice. "Take a look behind you. That's my crew coming up, and they're just as rough as you boys. Maybe a mite rougher. Besides, the Indians like this man. I rather suspicion they'd lift a scalp or two if anything happened to him."

The whisky peddlers continued to growl and complain, but they sheathed their knives at last and went back to the *Antelope*. Captain La Barge thanked his men and told them he didn't expect any more trouble.

"I owe you a great debt," said Father De Smet. He threw down the ax, only then realizing how far his zeal and anger had carried him. "I might have had their blood to answer for."

"Or they might have had yours," the captain answered gravely. "It's a tough country, this frontier; there are men in it worse than the wolves and the grizzlies. And you're lucky if you don't have to pay for that cask," he ended with a smile.

"I couldn't help myself. When I saw them rolling out that poison, and not a hand raised to stop them—"

"It's the agent's job to see that they don't sell it."

"The agent!" The priest's voice was scornful. "You know better, Joe. He's nothing but a bag of political wind. So long as he gets his salary and whatever pickings he can get from the traders, he'll never open his mouth. The Indians can drink themselves to death for all he cares. And the government at Washington's no better.

"Three months ago, the *Wilmington* brought up fifty casks of brandy and landed them here. Four dollars a bottle the peddlers got for it. She was hardly out of sight before the whole tribe was in a frenzy. You know how even one dram of firewater will drive an Indian off his head. I watched all our work undone in a single night. Women were putting their babies up for sale for a bottle. Next day the braves started fighting among themselves, maiming, killing. They sold their guns, their blankets, everything they owned for a drink.

"Weeks later, with more than thirty dead and Heaven only

knows how many more maimed for life, the chiefs came to the agent and begged him to keep the whisky sellers off the reservation. He's done nothing. I wrote twice to Washington, complaining about the failure to enforce the law. I never got even an answer. And you expect me to stand idle?"

"It's shameful, I'll admit. But can one man stop it?"

"One man can try."

Captain La Barge shook his head doubtfully. He sympathized with the priest, for in spite of his hard life on the river he was known to be a thoroughly upright man. Still he knew how hopeless was the task to which Father De Smet had set himself. Money was money to most traders, no matter how dirty the means of getting it might be. And as far as the majority of white frontiersmen were concerned, the sooner the Indians were killed off—or killed themselves off—the better. It was whispered that men in high authority at Washington were of the same opinion.

The whisky sellers and the gamblers and the cheap-johns did a great business for the next few days. The agent made no attempt to interfere with them. And, when all the Indians' money was spent, they departed. Just as before, there were murders and savage quarrels, and the trouble continued long after the traders had left. The braves sat in their tipis staring at nothing; a complete apathy seemed to have taken hold of them after the brief orgy. The farms were left untended. The outlook for the winter was grim and promised famine.

Father De Smet saw little reason to hope for any improvement. Even if the tribe managed to get through the winter, the same dismal scenes would be repeated when the next distribution day came. He had still received no replies from Washington, so it was plain that the whisky peddlers and gamblers could come and go as they pleased.

Only the little children gave any consolation to the missionaries. They were eager to learn and quick of mind, but in the dirt and squalor of the villages many of them died early of disease or neglect. It was well that God willed it so, thought Father De Smet. What chance did they have in a world where everything seemed against them?

At the darkest moment of his discouragement, however, something happened that was to give him and his brother missionaries a great new opportunity. About the middle of September 1839 two strange Indians stopped at the mission and asked for food and shelter. They were delighted to find Black Robes there. They told the priests that they had been sent by their tribe to ask the chief Black Robe in St. Louis for one of his men who might teach them the word of God. Their tribe was called the Flatheads by the whites; they lived in the snowy mountains far to the westward.

The elder of these dark ambassadors in fringed leggings and buckskin jackets was Peter Left Hand; Ignatius was the younger of the two. They were fine-looking men, average in height but strongly built; their physical condition and bright, fearless eyes were in strong contrast to the flabbiness and beaten looks of the Potawatomis.

Their mission to St. Louis had a simple explanation. Many years before, they said, a band of Caughnawaga Iroquois had left their homes near Montreal to venture into the Far West. The Flathead tribe had received them like brothers, and so they had settled down in the heart of the Rocky Mountains and were now one with the Flatheads. The old Iroquois chief had gone to a Jesuit school in Canada. He had never ceased urging the Flatheads and their neighbors, the Pend d'Oreilles and the Nez Percés, to send for a Black Robe who would show them the way to a better life. Meanwhile, he had taught them to pray.

Three times the Flatheads had sent runners eastward to ask for a priest. Three times the messengers had come to grief and no Black Robe had been sent. Now, this fourth time, perhaps their wish would be granted.

The missionaries gave them letters to the Bishop, and to the Jesuit Superior in St. Louis, and they went on their way. "If only my health might permit it," wrote Father De Smet to his brother, telling him of the incident, "I might have the luck this time to get farther up the Missouri. Should God think me worthy of the honor, I'd willingly give my life to help these Indians."

Meanwhile, Peter Left Hand and Ignatius got safely to St. Louis and were assured by the Bishop that a Black Robe would go to the Flathead country in the spring. Peter set off at once to carry the great news to the tribe, but Ignatius stayed to accompany the priest who would be selected for the long and dangerous journey.

Who would that priest be? As soon as Father De Smet learned that the Bishop wanted a Jesuit to go, he made up his mind that only one Jesuit would do. He dinned away at Father Verhaegen, his Superior, until the assignment was promised him. With high hopes, he made his preparations for the great adventure.

Chapter 3

THE COUNTRY OF THE FLATHEADS

On May 7, 1840, after a week on the trail from Westport, Missouri, a trading party of the American Fur Company was making its way toward the Platte River country. At the head of the line of two-wheeled carts and laden pack mules rode the captain of the caravan, alert for thieving Indians and trouble of any kind. He wore deerskin trousers and a white blanket coat; his long knife was stuck in his belt, his bullet pouch and powder horn swung by his side, and his rifle rested on the high pommel of his saddle. Behind him, the teamsters cracked their whips and shouted at their animals in French, English, and half-a-dozen Indian tongues.

At the very end of the caravan, stretched out in a cart and racked with chills and fever, lay the new missionary to the Flathead Indians, Father De Smet. His sickness had come on him suddenly; he had tried to sit his horse and fight it, but the continued attacks had weakened him to the point of dizziness. The captain had ordered the priest to ride in the cart. Regardless of how anyone might feel, the caravan had to keep moving and the discipline was strict.

Father De Smet and his guide Ignatius, who, dressed in fringed leggings and a buckskin shirt, rode anxiously beside him, had joined the fur company's party because it was the safest and surest means of reaching the valley of Green River in the heart of the Rockies. This was the place where the

Flatheads had arranged to meet the promised Black Robe.

There, every year, the trappers and Indians came in from the mountains to trade. They exchanged their packs of furs for gunpowder and lead, for new beaver traps and Mackinaw blankets, for tobacco, fishhooks, knives and all else that was needful. This carnival in the mountains was called *the rendezvous.*

For the first day or two, the way to the Far West had seemed easy. The trail rolled gently across the Kansas prairies, the air was clear and springlike, and Father De Smet was filled with a sense of high adventure. At last he was to do the work for which he had left his family and his country; the dreams of his boyhood were about to become realities.

When the trail swung northwest, however, they had come to a somber and lonely country broken by many, many creeks and rivers. The going grew hard. They forded some of the rivers without much trouble, but at others they had to lower the carts down into deep ravines on ropes and haul them up the opposite banks by sheer human strength. The prairie was already boggy with the spring rains, and then thunderstorms broke on them without warning, washing out the camp or pelting the moving column with snow and hail. Ignatius and the teamsters said that the sodden plains would be beautiful with waving grass and flowers in another three weeks, but it was hard to believe.

Each morning, at sunrise, the horses were brought back from the picket line and the balky mules were rounded up and packed. Then it was off again, to the music of creaking saddle leather and the shouting and swearing of the teamsters. They rested at midday—"nooning" as it was called—and a guard was posted, just as at night. The Pawnees, whose country they had reached, wouldn't dare attack a group of thirty armed men but a careful captain of a party took nothing for granted on the way westward.

After the "nooning" the caravan pushed on, always at the same pace, until late afternoon. Then camp was made and the animals were herded out to graze. At twilight, the drivers tethered the horses and mules. Then the night guard was set, the mess was eaten by the fire, and there was sleep. The air at night was very cold.

Thanks to the simple remedies he took and to Ignatius' constant care, Father De Smet's fever began to lessen. On the 18th of May he roused himself to see the "coasts of the Nebraska" looming in the distance—the high bluffs that bound the valley of the Platte River. For many, many miles, the trail was to follow this wide and shallow stream. It wound past the islands blooming with flowers and cottonwoods that dotted the Platte past "prairie-dog towns" or long lines of burrows each with its little brown-and-white occupant standing sentinel at the entrance, past the lonely graves of Pawnee warriors raised up on poles above the ground to protect the bodies from the wolves.

They met buffalo for the first time just east of the place where the Platte forked and the trail cut over to the river's northern branch. For some time they'd noticed painted skulls and bones arranged in careful patterns on the plains. These were called "medicine circles"; the Indians set them out as offerings to the buffalo spirit. Now the party came on a full herd of the huge and clumsy beasts. The men of the caravan shouted with joy and prepared for a hunt.

Father De Smet was still very weak, but he climbed a bluff beside the river and watched Ignatius and the others gallop in among the thousands of grazing animals. The herd thundered off in wild flight but not before a number had

fallen. The hunters took the tongues, the humps and the rib meat for their own use. They left the rest for the buzzards and the wolves.

What a strange life he was leading, thought the priest! It was like the wanderings of the ancient peoples of whom the Bible told, when cattle reposed on a thousand hills and man never lost sight of God's provident care.

After the caravan forded the south branch of the Platte and crossed to the north, the voyagers came to a barren and treeless country. It was cut and seamed by deep ravines and the dry beds of one-time streams. The grade of this wide valley rose steadily upward. The grass was short and patchy, drinking water grew scarce, and the Platte flowed shallow, sluggish and bitter with alkali between numberless islands nodding with cottonwoods. Here, in what the men called the high plains, the sun beat down pitilessly; the dust rose around the travelers in clouds. But Father De Smet felt stronger every day. The fever had left him.

Buttes and mesas, carved by wind and sand into a thousand fantastic shapes, rose up beside the trail. Some of them seemed like buildings raised by giants; one looked like a tall chimney. Still at the steady pace that had brought them five hundred miles without disaster, the caravan toiled up and down the gullies and ravines until the broken hills drew together into long ridges. The trail left the river at that point and wandered, seemingly aimless, among looming cliffs and bleak, barren rocks. Wild horses coursed by, and big-horn sheep looked down on the caravan from the high crags. Rattlesnakes were everywhere.

On the 4th of June, for the first time in many days, they encountered other human beings. They reached Fort Laramie, the fur company's famous trading post, which lay in a narrow valley enclosed by grassy hills. It was a large blockhouse built of cottonwood logs. On three sides of the fifteen-foot wall were little towers for watch and defense. Inside, a number of small, flat-roofed buildings huddled like swallows' nests against the wall. These were the storehouses and the dwellings of the garrison. The central courtyard was used as a horse pen.

Five men were on duty at the fort and they gave the travelers a hearty welcome. The captain and the men of the caravan were soon deep in talk over the state of trade with the Sioux and the Crows, but Father De Smet and Ignatius went to visit a camp of Cheyennes who had set up their lodges (tents made of skins) a short distance from the fort.

"My heart is glad," said the Cheyenne chief, after Ignatius had explained who the priest was. "We have heard of the Black Robes who talk with the Great Spirit. We have never seen one until now. My lodge has never known a greater day."

The chief and the missionary smoked the ceremonial pipe of peace, the calumet; and then, for the first time, Father De Smet preached to the people of the plains. He explained what the Creed meant, and how God loved mankind, and the purpose of the Ten Commandments. As Ignatius translated his words, the Cheyennes listened with the greatest attention. When he had finished, they broke their silence with deep grunts of satisfaction.

"Your words are good," said the chief. "Stay with us."

"I cannot," the priest replied. "I have promised to go to the mountains. But another will come—maybe next year—"

At sunrise the caravan left Fort Laramie. Now the mountains were always in view—at first a single peak, and then a misty mass like a great wall against the far horizon. The broken land through which the trail passed was gay with wild flowers at first but it soon grew arid. They came at last to a rocky desert. Here they left the valley of the Platte and crossed over to another river, the Sweetwater, which ran down from the mighty Rockies. The men's tempers were short, for the road to the Sweetwater wound about amid greasewood, sagebrush and alkali sand, and it was increasingly steep.

A chain of the Rockies was clearly visible on their right; it looked to Father De Smet like the ruins of a world. Rock towered over snow-crowned rock in a vast confusion.

"The Wind River Mountains," Ignatius said. "We reach Green River in nine days—maybe eight. Peter Left Hand and my brothers will be there. They will be glad."

Colder and colder grew the air. On the 24th of June the caravan crossed plains which were dusted with snow, and on the following day they were in the South Pass—the broad plateau which led over the top of the continent. It was a sagebrush-covered plain about twenty miles wide, and seemed less like a pass than a dip between the southernmost peaks of the Wind River range and the badlands southward of them. For two days thereafter they toiled across a flat of alkali sand over which the wind swept ceaselessly. Then they descended the valley of the Big Sandy to the lower valley of the Green.

About twenty-five miles north of where the Big Sandy came in, the Green River broke rapid and clear through a range of hills. On June 30 the trading party reached the crest of these hills and looked out over the upper valley. They had been sixty days on the trail and their goal was in sight. Fifty miles long and from thirty to seventy miles wide, the upper valley of the Green was barren and treeless except for lines of cottonwoods that waved along the river's course and beside the creeks that fed the river from both east and west. Flights of ducks and geese skimmed by in patterns of cold and lonely beauty against the sky. Bounding the valley on either side rose the heavily wooded flanks of the mountains.

"Dress up!" shouted the captain, swinging round in his saddle and frowning at the straggling line of carts and mules. "Let's look smart when we ride into camp."

Father De Smet saw only a sprawl of makeshift huts and Indian lodges well to the northward, where a fairly large creek flowed into the river and formed a fertile delta.

"Is that *the rendezvous*?" he asked.

"Aye, up there by Horse Creek," answered the captain glumly. "Not much to see, is it? Ten years ago—or five, even— you'd have seen lodges for miles on both sides of the river. You'd have heard the shoutin' and singin' all the way from Big Sandy. There was fun in them days. Yarnin' and drinkin' for a week, day and night—wrasslin' games and shootin' at marks! Why, I've seen the time when a mountain man'd lose five hundred dollars on the turn of one card. But the beaver trade ain't what it was, and this'll be the last rendezvous if business ain't better'n last year. Maybe we'd all better go down Oregon way and take up farms."

By this time the caravan had been sighted, and about three hundred horsemen came galloping out from the camp to welcome the traders. They were mostly Shoshone Indians in full paint and armed with clubs. They rode up whooping, and waving long poles decorated with scalps. They boasted loudly of their many brave deeds in war.

Attended by this loud cavalry, the trading party arrived soon afterward at the camp. Lean, bearded, white mountain men crowded around the carts; Indian bucks in leggings and shirts, wearing necklaces of bear and wolf claws; squaws in deerskin tunics black with grease but tricked out with ribbons, fur and foofaraw of every kind. The huckstering and horseplay began at once.

Ignatius led Father De Smet to the northern end of the encampment where several lodges were set up at a little distance from the others. A small group of Indians stood waiting there; the priest recognized Peter Left Hand among them.

"These are my brothers," said Ignatius. "Big Face, our chief, sent them to bring you safely to our country."

Father De Smet greeted each man, and his eyes filled with happy tears. He was not ashamed of it; why shouldn't he show them that he wanted to be their friend? He would love these savage men because they were children of God and made in His image. Whatever he could do for them, he would do.

The Indians seemed to read his heart. Their solemn, dark faces broke into delighted smiles. They all began to talk at once, some welcoming him to their tribe, others telling of a marvelous adventure they'd had on their way to the rendezvous.

"We were few," they said, "and the Blackfeet were many. For five days we fought them. But the Great Spirit knew that we were coming to meet you; He took pity on us. The Blackfeet lost many warriors. They went away weeping."

Father De Smet rested for several days before setting out for the Flathead country. On Sunday, July 3, he built an altar on a little hill covered with wild flowers and said Mass. The Canadian trappers at *the rendezvous* sang hymns in French and Latin, and many curious white men stood silently by; but the Indians seemed to know by instinct the sacred character of the ceremony. They gathered close around the altar and chanted prayers in their own languages to the Master of Life.

Next day the Flatheads broke camp. The main body of the tribe, together with their neighbors and relatives the Pend d'Oreilles, were awaiting their Black Robe in a valley many miles to the northward where there was better forage for the horse herd than at *the rendezvous*. Their homeland was the valley of the Bitter Root, but like all western Indians whose living depended on hunting they were accustomed to wander from place to place—men, women and children, horses and dogs.

For several days Ignatius, Peter Left Hand and the others followed the course of the Green River; then they crossed over westward and went up a mountain stream to a high plain bright with flax flowers. A narrow trail led from this plain down through a gorge of frightening depth and upward again over the shoulder of a mountain heavily wooded with cedar, fir and pine. Soon their way was barred by a torrent in full flood, roaring over granite boulders and throwing up high plumes of foam. The Flatheads said it was the Snake River. They rode their horses fearlessly into the water and swam to the other side. Father De Smet was afraid to try this way of crossing, so the Indians showed him how to make a boat by stuffing out his deerskin tent with his baggage and tying the loose ends together on top. This strange device floated like a swan. He seated himself on it, and the swimming Indians guided it across the river in ten minutes.

Next day they rode through thick pine forests until they came to a pass—Teton Pass, it was called—from which they descended by a steep, slippery trail to a very beautiful valley.

"The people are here," said Ignatius. "I will ride ahead to tell them that their father has come."

Father De Smet felt very humble as he watched Ignatius ride off. Other missionaries had had to labor for years among uncivilized men before they could win so much as a hearing, but he was called to a people who were anxious to hear the Gospel.

The combined camp of the Flatheads and Pend d'Oreilles was a large one—three hundred lodges or more, pitched in fair order on both sides of a stream. As the priest and his guides came in sight of it, hundreds of Indians ran toward them, shouting a welcome and leaping for joy. They led Father De Smet at once to the chief's lodge, where Big Face sat among all his councillors.

"You are welcome in my nation, Black Robe," the chief began, after gazing a long time at the priest from black eyes, deep-set in a stern, very wrinkled face. "Today our hearts are big. Kaikolinzoeten [the Great Spirit] has granted our wishes. You've come to a poor people, an ignorant people, too—yet I've taught my children to love the Great Spirit. The poles of your lodge are already set up, and we shall follow the words of your mouth."

He stood up and motioned to the priest to take his place at the head of the council.

"I thank you," replied Father De Smet, "but I cannot take your place. I have not come to rule you, or to change the ways of your fathers. Later, perhaps, you may think it wise to settle in one place which suits you and is fertile. If you learn to take your living from the earth, you can escape the hungry times and defend yourselves better against your enemies. I will teach you how to do this if you wish it, but for the present I shall talk to you only of God."

He told them then what times he thought would be best for prayers and for instruction. Big Face and his councillors nodded their heads in agreement with all he said.

Next morning, at daybreak, Big Face galloped through the camp, rousing his people from sleep and calling on them to wash themselves in the river and hasten to the Black Robe's lodge.

"Be quiet when you get there," he cried. "Open your ears and your hearts to him. Hold fast everything he says to you." The Flatheads were quick to obey. Even the sick came, carried on litters by their friends. What a lesson this would be for the people of Europe, thought Father De Smet as he looked out at the many eager faces. Most white men thought they did a great deal for God when they came once a week to Mass, and late at that.

The Flatheads remained in their valley camp for almost a week, and each day Father De Smet gave instructions on the Creed, the Commandments and the Sacraments. Several of the Indians acted as interpreters and helped him translate the morning and evening prayers into their language. He used simple words in his talks and he never said too much at any one time. Whenever he paused, the listening Indians would light their pipes and talk among themselves about what they'd just heard. Then they would ask questions, and he would answer them.

These forest people had an honesty and innocence that put so-called civilized people to shame. When he explained that gambling displeased God because it showed a desire to possess other people's goods without working for them, the chiefs and the people voted to forbid it in their nation.

They had many virtues already. They considered a liar a criminal; theft was unknown among them; and any brave who started a quarrel in camp was severely punished. Like all Indians, the Flatheads were hospitable and friendly to any stranger who came in peace—but woe to anyone whom they caught trying to deceive or cheat them. They were very brave in war. Even the Sioux and the Blackfeet feared them.

The party left the valley about the twentieth of July and traveled slowly up Henry's Fork of the Snake River. Mountains towered on all sides of the trail. Some were cone-shaped, wooded and capped with snow; others were reddish in hue, naked of trees and shaped like flattened domes. The grass was high in the valleys and flowers were everywhere. Mountain balsam, crushed under the feet of the horses, scented the clear air.

When they reached Henry's Lake, one of the sources of the westward-flowing Columbia River, Father De Smet climbed a nearby mountain and looked down upon Red Rock Lake to the eastward, from which a principal fork of the Missouri flowed. Here in the high places, just as in the vast plains, he was filled with joy in the grandeur of God's creation. Kneeling down, he prayed that he might do his work well.

The dream of a second Paraguay was not impossible. The

few weeks he had spent among the Flatheads proved that these so-called savage peoples were hungry for a knowledge of God and most worthy to receive it. Already they were talking of the place where they would settle. Only hard work and God's grace were needed to turn these glorious valleys into fertile farms on which a simple Christian people could grow in prosperity and perfection.

Moved by a sudden impulse, Father De Smet took his knife and carved on the soft rock beside him: *Saint Ignatius— Patron of the Mountains—July 23, 1840.* It was at once a dedication and a prayer.

His wandering life continued. Sometimes the tribe set up its lodges in open, smiling valleys ; at other times it roamed through narrow and perilous passes on to high, rocky plains, desert-like in their barren loneliness. Each morning the priest said Mass at an altar of willows; his blanket was the altar cloth. Around him knelt the Indians, reciting their prayers in the Flathead, Nez Perce and Iroquois tongues.

Late in August they came to a broad plain where three rivers joined; it was the celebrated Three Forks, at which the Jefferson, Gallatin and Madison rivers united to form the Missouri. The Indians were happy to find the plain covered with grazing buffalo. They'd been living very well on elk and deer meat since they'd left Green River, but the tribe had always to think of winter supplies as well as present food. So on sight of the buffalo herds they hastened to set up willow racks for drying the meat, and prepared their bows and lances for a great hunt.

Four hundred Flatheads and Pend d'Oreilles mounted their best horses and, at a signal from one of the chiefs, rode at top speed among the buffalo. The chase seemed aimless at first, but Father De Smet soon realized that the hunters were picking out the fattest cows from among the fleeing animals. In three hours they'd killed more than five hundred beasts. Then the old men, the women and the children came with lodgepole drags to carry away the carcasses, and in a very short time the willow racks were full. There was no longer any fear of a hungry winter.

Father De Smet had already told Big Face and the other chiefs that he was under orders to return to St. Louis before fall. God willing, he'd return in the spring to be their Black Robe, and bring other Black Robes with him perhaps; but now he must go and tell his superiors what he had found in the mountain country.

Long before sunrise on the day of his departure the people gathered outside his lodge to bid him farewell in their own way. Not a word was said, but every dark face looked grieved. As he led them in the morning prayer, many of them burst into tears. He thanked them for their kindness to him and begged them to serve the Great Spirit faithfully while he was gone.

"We will pray for you night and morning," replied Big Face. "Now, our hearts are sad—but when the snow melts in the valleys we will begin to be happy again. When the grass grows green, our joy will be greater. And when the flowers appear, your children of the mountains will come to meet you."

Chapter 4

WILDERNESS ADVENTURES

You must look at the map if you are to get any idea of Father De Smet's travels during the next four months. From the camp on the Three Forks he and the warriors and war chiefs who had come with him crossed the Yellowstone River and followed it to a trading post of the American Fur Company called Fort Alexander. Here, the Black Robe insisted that the Flathead guides return to the mountains.

"We've come where your enemies are strong—the Blackfeet, the Assiniboine, the Sioux," he said. "You've risked

43

your lives already for my sake, and every mile farther will mean a greater risk. You're needed at home, and God will protect me."

He had to argue a long time with them before they were persuaded to leave him. Then, with only a single companion, he continued down the Yellowstone Valley for ten days, until he saw rising out of the plain ahead of him the tall blockhouses of Fort Union. This trading post lay just above the junction of the Yellowstone with the Missouri River.

The traders at the fort were amazed to see the Black Robe. It seemed a miracle to them that a white man could have ridden down the Yellowstone in safety through country thick with warring Indians. A friendly Sioux at the fort had a simple explanation for it. "You are close to the Great Spirit," he said. "He sent His *manitous* [good spirits] to watch over you."

Three of the fur company's employees accompanied Father De Smet on the next stage of his journey to St. Louis—to the villages inhabited by the Mandan, Gros Ventre and Aricara tribes. The land through which they traveled was more fertile than the arid, gravelly land around the Yellowstone, but it was still a vast prairie studded with occasional high hills and crisscrossed with dry gulches and ravines. The grass was burned brown and there was barely enough fodder for the horses.

The approach to the Mandan villages was gruesome. The travelers were riding close to the river when they came to a small forest. Tied high among the branches of the trees were hundreds of corpses wrapped in buffalo hides. It was a cemetery, said the fur company men. Only a few years before an epidemic of smallpox had ravaged the Mandans and Aricaras and almost wiped them out. The remnants of the tribes had joined up with the Gros Ventres of the prairies.

At the Mandan villages Father De Smet attended as many as twenty banquets a day. He did not eat at all of them, however, for by Indian custom a guest could refuse food if he offered it to another person with a small present of tobacco. From there he hastened on to Fort Pierre, the principal trading center for the Sioux nation. The fur company men stayed with the Mandans, but a Canadian trapper went along with the Black Robe and it was fortunate that he did.

Three days down the Missouri from the Mandan villages a band of Indians came galloping round a butte and took them completely by surprise. It was a war party of Santee Sioux. Far from harming the two white men, the Sioux gave them food. The Canadian trapper was frightened by the meeting, however, and from that time he and Father De Smet rode in the bottom of ravines so as not to be seen from any distance. This strategy worked well for two days, but on the third day, as they were camped beside a spring, a yelling band of red men rode over the crest of the hill above them and made them prisoners.

"Blackfeet Sioux," called out the trapper. "Bad!"

Father De Smet was dragged over to the chief. He held up his hand in the peace sign, but the chief paid no attention.

"Why are you hiding here?" he demanded.

"We were tired and hungry. The water of the spring was good."

"I have never seen a man in clothes like these," said the chief, turning to the Canadian trapper. "What kind of man is this?" He was staring at the priest's ragged cassock and the large missionary crucifix which he wore in his belt.

"He is a servant of the Great Spirit," the Canadian answered.

The chief's fierce frown relaxed. He spoke a few words to his men, then he put out his hand in friendship. Father De Smet made them all a present of some tobacco and they smoked the peace pipe together.

The chief invited Father De Smet and the trapper to spend the night in his own village which was close by. A buffalo hide was laid on the ground, and the Black Robe was asked to sit down. To his astonishment twelve Indians seized the robe by its edges, lifted it in the air, and carried him in triumph to the village. It was a large camp, and the priest thought it looked very gay. The hundred or more lodges were painted with figures of deer, buffalo and other animals in bright red, yellow and orange.

Forty warriors were present at the evening feast in the chief's lodge, where Father De Smet was given the place of honor. When he crossed himself and began to say grace, the Indians raised their hands aloft, lowering them to the ground when he had finished. He explained what his prayer meant, and then asked them the meaning of their gesture.

"It is our custom, Black Robe," the chief answered. "We raise our hands because we owe the Great Spirit everything. He gives us what we need. We strike the ground afterward because we are only worms crawling before His face."

Later that night, as Father De Smet lay in his tent, a rustling noise outside disturbed him. He sat up. As he did so, a dark figure glided in. A strong hand seized his arm and he felt a knife blade pressing against his throat.

"Are you afraid, Black Robe?" growled a voice. It was the chief's voice.

The priest said nothing. He took the chief's hand and put it against his own breast. Then he asked calmly:

"Does my heart beat faster than usual? That will answer

you. Why should I be afraid? You have taken me into your own lodge and fed me. I'm as safe here as I would be in my father's house."

The chief was delighted with the reply. He had come only to test his guest's courage and confidence in him. He swore friendship with Father De Smet, and when the white men were ready to journey on he sent his son with them to guide them safely to Fort Pierre.

It was fine, clear October weather when they reached the fort; the last stage of the journey to St. Louis lay ahead, and it should have been an easy one. But the horses gave out just before they reached Fort Vermillion and they had to take to the river in a canoe. Soon the weather turned cold and the Missouri was filled with floating ice. The prairie had been burned over on either bank, so there was no game to be hunted for food. For many days they fought their way downstream through ice floes and vicious snags, eating only frozen potatoes and a little dried meat.

On the very day the river froze up solid, they reached the Potawatomi mission and rested at last among friends. Father Christian Hoecken and Father Verreydt marveled at their brother Jesuit's adventures and were delighted to hear his glowing account of the Flatheads and the Pend d'Oreilles. They had little good to report of the Potawatomis, however; those unfortunates were even worse off than they'd been the year before.

After a few days' rest Father De Smet set off overland through the reservations of the Otoes, Iowas, Sauks and Delawares, and reached Westport on the night of December 22. Next morning he took the stagecoach at the town of Independence, Missouri, and arrived in St. Louis on the eve of the New Year, burning with impatience to tell his superiors all that he'd seen and of his high hopes for a second Paraguay in the western mountains.

Father Provincial was pleased to hear that the Flatheads and the Pend d'Oreilles were so well grounded in the Faith, but he opened his eyes wide at Father De Smet's plans for a mission which would also educate the northwest tribes in the arts of peace.

"We're deep in debt already," he protested. "And we haven't a man to spare."

Yet when the missionary set out in the spring of 1841, to keep his appointment with the Flatheads, he was accompanied by two priests and three skilled lay brothers, and he had money enough to keep the work going for the first year. The zeal of the Jesuits had provided the men. The money had been raised by begging letters, written to bishops, priests and laymen all over the United States. Father De Smet had succeeded in arousing much of his own enthusiasm for the work among the people there. Women had given him their jewels; even the slaves had come to him with the little they had to contribute.

St. Mary's Mission was soon under construction in the valley of the Bitterroot River. The Flatheads themselves chose the place. Great jagged mountains hemmed in the valley on all sides; the narrow pass that led into it could be defended easily against raiding Blackfeet. Pine, fir, willows and cottonwoods grew in profusion along the river's course and there was plenty of grass for the animals, but Brother Claessens thought that the soil was a little light for farming.

Once they made up their minds to settle down and live as the white men lived, the Flatheads labored with a will. Five weeks after work was begun on the mission village, several buildings were up and in usable condition. The village had been surrounded by a strong stockade.

Each day began with the sound of the Angelus bell. Then Mass was said, instructions were given to the adult Indians, and the Jesuits visited the sick. The children came for catechism classes at two o'clock each afternoon. Each evening the whole tribe gathered to recite the evening prayers together. It seemed to the missionaries that the days of the early Church had been renewed, so eager were the Indians to learn and practice their religion, to be baptized, and to receive the Holy Eucharist.

As farmers, the Flatheads didn't progress quite so rapidly— but a people who had always lived by hunting and fishing couldn't be expected to change their habits overnight. When Brother Claessens showed them how to plant seeds, they told him that it was stupid to put good food in the ground where it would only rot. The first fine crop of wheat, oats and potatoes had to appear before the tribesmen believed the Black Robes' story that the earth of their own valley could give them all the food they needed.

Father De Smet, as Superior of the mission, had to make several long journeys in search of farm tools, clothing and seeds. He went first to Fort Colville, a post of the Hudson's Bay Company which lay some three hundred miles northwest of St. Mary's. His second trip was to Fort Vancouver, the trading center for the whole Northwest, a thousand miles to the westward at the junction of the Columbia and the Willamette rivers. As he traveled through the wilderness, sometimes overland in the snow, sometimes by boat down the rushing flood of the Columbia, he lost no opportunity of seeking out new tribes and preaching to them. In this way he brought the Gospel to the Kalispels, the Kootenais, the Okanagans, the Chaudieres and the Coeur d'Alènes. Some of these tribes had heard of Christianity from wandering Iroquois or from the Canadian trappers who traded with them, but Father De Smet was the first Black Robe who had ever come to them.

"For a long time we have wished to see you, Black Robe," said the chief of the Coeur d'Alènes. "Our fathers prayed to the sun and the earth. I remember very well when we first heard of the one true God. Since that time we have prayed to Him, but we never knew the words of the Great Spirit. All is still darkness with us, but today I hope we shall see the light shine."

"Never have I seen more convincing proofs of sincere conversion to God," wrote Father De Smet about his visit to the Coeur d'Alènes.

"Not even when I met the Flatheads in 1840."

It was no wonder, then, that he promised all these tribes missions of their own like St. Mary's, and Black Robes to teach and serve them. Where the priests and lay brothers were to be found, or where the necessary money was to come from, he didn't know—but with God's aid nothing was impossible.

While he was at Fort Vancouver in the summer of 1842, he met two remarkable men: the famous Dr. John McLoughlin, and Father Francois Norbert Blanchet, a Canadian priest who was later to be the first bishop in Oregon. Father Blanchet was pastor at the fort and he also served the many Canadians who had taken up land for farming along the Willamette River. Dr. McLoughlin was the man in charge of all the activities of the Hudson's Bay Company in the Northwest.

Both the priest and the businessman were delighted to hear of the founding of St. Mary's, but they told Father De Smet that the Jesuits should go even further in their planning. The education of the Indians was all very well, and a noble work, but Oregon would soon be full of white people who would need schools and a college, too. The tide of new immigrants from Canada and the United States was rising; in a few years it would be at flood. They were troubled that no provision was being made for the education of the immigrants' children.

Father De Smet was troubled in mind on his thirty-day journey back to St. Mary's with the load of spades, hoes, carpenter's tools and clothing that he'd purchased at Fort Vancouver. Someone would have to speak in behalf of the Northwest tribes, so eager for conversion and education, and for the white settlers also. Father Blanchet had even talked of a school for girls, to be taught by nuns! Where would a congregation of nuns be found who were willing to brave the wilderness? Who would persuade them to come and provide the means for their journey? Who could convince Father Provincial at St. Louis, or Father General at Rome, that the need and the opportunity in far western America demanded immediate action?

Late in July Father De Smet arrived back in the valley of the Bitterroot. The young men had left the village for the summer hunt, and Father De Smet traveled after them to the Three Forks of the Missouri. By the time he reached the hunting camp, he'd made his decision. He would leave St. Mary's in the capable hands of one of his assistant priests, Father Gregory Mengarini; he would send Father Nicholas Point and Brother Huet to start a new mission village among the Coeur d'Alènes.

As for himself, much as he disliked the idea, he would have to turn beggar again. If his superiors approved of his plans, the whole United States—and Europe, too—would hear about the worthiness and the needs of the mountain Indians. Those he couldn't reach with his voice, he'd reach with his pen. He'd already written begging letters to good purpose; now he'd write books, tracts, newspaper articles— anything that would carry the message. Nor would he forget the Oregon settlers.

Father De Smet crossed the now familiar Yellowstone country to the Missouri and descended that great river to Westport, arriving at St. Louis on the last Sunday of October. There was no withstanding the appeal of a man who'd traveled almost five thousand miles since the spring of the year, and now asked only for permission to fare further in God's cause. Father Provincial consented to the begging campaign. He also sent two priests and a lay brother to help Father Mengarini and Father Point.

Soon the people of New Orleans were listening to the moving story of St. Mary's and pledging their aid; in swift succession Father De Smet spoke at Baltimore, Philadelphia, New York and Boston. His first book, *Letters and Sketches, with a Narrative of a Year's Residence among the Indian Tribes of the Rocky Mountains,* appeared from a Philadelphia publishing house and was widely read. On the seventh of June, 1843, he sailed for Europe.

His trip was a brilliant success. The people of Holland, Ireland and Belgium were generous with their money and with all kinds of useful articles. In Rome, Father Roothaan, the General of the Jesuits, called on several of the provinces of the Society for volunteers to staff the mountain missions and to make a beginning in Oregon. Gregory XVI, the Holy Father himself, received Father De Smet in audience and praised his efforts.

The least likely of all his projects—a girls' school for Oregon—was assured. The Sisters of Notre Dame of Namur were sending six of their number to found it. When the happy Black Robe boarded the brig *Infatigable* at Antwerp for the long voyage around Cape Horn, five Jesuit volunteers and the new community of Sisters accompanied him.

The sun was bright, but waves were breaking with a sullen roar over the long bar and the hidden reefs that screened the southern entrance to the Columbia River.

For several days the *Infatigable's* captain had stood off and on while he tried to make a decision. Should he run through the breakers and land his passengers in Oregon? Or should he head out to sea again? The passage had been a wild one, and long. Off Cape Horn the gales had torn the furled sails from the yards; they had been becalmed so often between Callao and the North American coast that both food and drinking water were low.

Out ahead of the vessel, one of her boats rocked on the waves like a tiny wooden chip. The second mate was taking soundings, shouting back the depth of the water through his cupped hands.

"Seven fathoms," he called.

"I'll try it," said the captain suddenly to Father De Smet who stood anxiously beside him, his broad body braced. "This is a lucky ship. We'll get through."

Please God, thought the missionary as he looked ahead to the shore over the waste of white water. And by the intercession of St. Ignatius—for the day was his feast day—the 31st of July 1844.

The *Infatigable* moved slowly ahead in a light breeze.

"Seven fathoms," called the mate. Then, "Six fathoms—five—four—"

The captain looked grim but he gave no order to the helmsman. The ocean frothed and boiled on every side of them; the roar of the breakers was deafening. Three fathoms was the vessel's draft, thought Father De Smet. If the water shoaled much more the *Infatigable* would surely strike.

"Four fathoms—four—three!"

Father De Smet could hear the voices of the Sisters and his fellow Jesuits reciting the Rosary. They'd done that off Cape Horn when it seemed certain that the ship would be hurled to wreck on the wild coast of Patagonia. "Let God dispose of us as it seems good to Him," one of the Sisters had said then. So it should be now. Yet it would be a pity to fail now in sight of their goal. "St. Ignatius, our patron, help us!" he whispered.

"Three and a half!" The mate's voice was hoarse but hopeful. "Four—six—seven fathoms !"

"We're across the bar," shouted the captain, pounding Father De Smet vigorously on the back in his joy. "We're safe."

In a very short time they dropped anchor before Fort

George at Astoria. There they learned that no ship of their draft had ever before attempted the southern entrance to the river. For two days the men at the fort had been watching the *Infatigable,* hoping that she would escape an almost certain disaster.

The settlers along the Willamette had built a convent on the right bank of that river, so the Sisters were soon at home and busy. The Jesuits chose a good site for their house, dedicated it to St. Francis Xavier, and set to work on the buildings.

Father De Smet, after purchasing supplies at Fort Vancouver for St. Mary's and the new mountain missions, was anxious to set off and deliver them, but he was plagued with a new illness. The wilderness journeys and the constant labors of the past four years were taking their toll. He found himself subject to severe attacks of rheumatic pain, but nothing altered his kindly zeal.

Word came to Father Blanchet that the Holy Father had named him bishop of the Oregon territory. Father De Smet's face lit up when he heard the news. He'd heard talk in Rome that the honor was intended for himself but he'd pleaded with Father Roothaan to save him from a task for which he felt incapable and unworthy. Let other and more gifted men be the administrators; he was fit only to break the trails, to make the journeys, to beg for money.

Chapter 5

WINTER IN THE MOUNTAINS

Father De Smet returned to the mountains early in October. He reached Fort Walla Walla in fine weather, and then, after crossing the high plain to the Spokane River, he left his guides and pushed on alone to the prairie called "the Bay of the Kalispels."

As he entered the valley, bells rang and guns were shot off to welcome him. The Indians were overjoyed to see the Black Robe who had first visited them, and whose work was now carried on by Father Adrian Hoecken. They crowded around him, telling him of their plans to build a mission village, and listening to the advice he had for them. The mission was to be under the patronage of St. Ignatius.

Father De Smet stayed only two days with the Kalispels. Already it was November 8. He had to cross the Bitterroot range to St. Mary's before the heavy snows began. He made his preparations for crossing the mountains, but just as he was about to leave, messengers arrived from the Coeur d'Alènes. They had heard of his visit to their neighbors and asked if he meant to go off without visiting them. Rather than hurt their feelings, he promised to stop at Sacred Heart Mission—the name which had been chosen for the Coeur d'Alene village.

All the next day it snowed and rained; the trail along the flanks of the high hills grew slippery and treacherous. Father De Smet reached Sacred Heart Mission in a raging blizzard,

but he was glad he'd gone out of his way when he saw how pleased the Indians were. A few disputes had arisen between them and Father Point, but these were soon settled.

The weather grew worse and worse. He left the Coeur d'Alènes on November 19, and it was eight days before he and his Indian guides were able to get even to the foot of the mountains. While they were encamped there, two Nez Percés came to ask a night's shelter and some food. They gave such a fearsome account of the trails over the range that Father De Smet decided to return to Sacred Heart Mission in the morning. But this was easier said than done.

By morning each little brook they'd crossed had become a torrent of rushing water. The road back was one long misery of tumbles and drenchings. About halfway back they camped for the night beside a river. When they awoke, they found that the river had risen—water surrounded the camp on all sides. One of the Indians swam to dry land and carried the news of their plight to the mission. A rescue party of Coeur d'Alènes came in canoes and took the exhausted, half-frozen men on the final stage of their return to Sacred Heart.

Not the least discouraged, Father De Smet made another attempt to reach St. Mary's. Since the mountain trails were closed, he tried to ascend Clarks Fork of the Columbia River in a canoe. Ice soon blocked him. He was in the neighborhood of the Kalispels' winter camp, so he went there and asked for lodging until spring.

The Kalispels had not yet built a regular "reduction" or village, but their camp was as comfortable as a camp in the mountains could be. Their *tipis* were set up on a south slope so that the wind would blow the snow away from the surrounding bunch grass. They hoped that this ready forage would attract hungry game animals down from the mountains when the usual feeding places lay buried under the deep drifts. Groves of evergreens and cottonwoods sheltered the horse herd.

The *tipis* were all newly made and were tight and sound. Each family banked snow around the lower edge of their *tipi* to keep the wind out; the floors were packed hard; the willow-frame beds were snug with buffalo robes. If the game animals should prove scarce, there'd be pemmican to eat— dried meat, ground up fine and kept in *parfleches* (leather food bags) sealed with buffalo fat. But so long as the hunters could find fresh meat, the pot was kept stewing over the fire in the center of each *tipi*. It was flavored with roots, herbs and young buds dug out from under the snow. There were no fixed mealtimes. Whenever anyone felt hungry, he spooned out a portion from the steaming pot and ate.

The Kalispels had built a church of fir-tree logs and they

were very proud of it. They spent much of their time learning their prayers, listening to instructions, and asking questions. Father De Smet and Father Hoecken had few idle moments that winter.

After midnight Mass on Christmas Day, the tribe gathered for a feast. They were as joyous as a band of children. One hundred and twenty-four men and women had completed their instructions and were to be baptized in the morning, after the third Mass. As Father De Smet administered the Sacrament, repeating the ritual over each dark-skinned candidate, he felt that he'd never been so happy in his life.

"Receive this white garment," he said, over and over again, giving humble thanks to God in his own heart for making him the instrument of renewing so many souls. Only a little more than three years ago he'd stood on a mountaintop and dreamed of gathering these wandering, wild tribes into villages of self-supporting, peaceful Christians—just as the old-time Jesuits had done in Paraguay. And now Father De Smet's dream was coming true.

He saw in his imagination this same scene—kneeling, skin-clad figures, dark heads bowed to receive the water of Life—being repeated in prosperous Indian towns all the way from the Pacific to the Mississippi. He saw the many tribes—so full of native virtue and intelligence—growing in perfection and knowledge and civilization. A few years ago he had been alone; now thirteen of his brother Jesuits were working with him. A few years ago there had been barely enough money to pay his passage with the fur company's caravan; now Catholic America and Catholic Europe had heard his pleas and opened their hearts and their purses. In another ten years—

His happy mood changed at the thought. Already the

white man's shadow was darkening over the Northwest as more and more covered wagons creaked westward over the Oregon Trail. And along with the honest settlers, the scum and dregs of frontier America would flood in—the outlaws, the whisky peddlers, the swindling gamblers.

Could the mountain tribes keep the white garment of their Baptism unspotted when the white man's bad example was everywhere before their eyes? Or would they go the way of the Potawatomis, the Omahas and the Iowas, who lived from year to year for the government handout and the "big drunk"?

These are only savages, the whites would say—as they'd said before in Michigan and Wisconsin and Missouri. *Sweep them off their hunting grounds, for we need farms! Hunt them like vermin out of their valleys and their mountains!* Time— that was what Father De Smet needed, as much as men and money. Time to teach the Indians, to gather them into communities such as St. Mary's where they'd be fixed on the soil, to arm them—not with guns and knives, but with the more lasting weapons of reason, knowledge and law. If he could do so, the trespassing whites would raise their voices in vain.

There could be no rest, he thought, as he walked back to his lodge that bright Christmas morning. Each day, each minute must be made to count.

On a fine afternoon early in the spring of 1851 Father John Elet, the new Superior of the Jesuits in the Missouri Province, sat in his office at St. Louis talking with a distinguished visitor. The visitor was Colonel David Mitchell, the Superintendent of Indian Affairs, and he had something important on his mind.

"If the scheme works," the Colonel was saying, "there'll be a lasting peace out there. We're sending word that we'll meet the Indians at Laramie in September."

"It sounds like a fine plan, Colonel."

"Don't give me any credit for it. It's Tom Fitzpatrick's idea." The Colonel got up from his shiny leather chair and grasped the lapels of his frock coat as he paced up and down the small office.

"He's our agent with the Sioux, Arapaho and Cheyenne—they call him Broken Hand. He's honest and they trust him. He's traded with them for years, and with most of the tribes along the high plains and in the mountains. Well, Tom's been telling us for a long time that they'll make war unless the government pays 'em for the buffalo that've been killed along the Platte. The Oregon emigrants and the California gold rushers have wasted more grass and killed more buffalo in five years than all the Indians have since time began. Why don't we do right by the Indians, says Tom, before they go on the warpath and make us do right?"

"The grass and the buffalo are the Indians' living," agreed Father Elet. "They'd starve without them, the way things stand now."

"That's true. When a settler grazes his oxen or shoots a beast out there, the Indians figure that he's stealing their property. Well, Congress has decided to pay them damages and that's why we're calling a big council. And now I'll come to the point. I want Father De Smet to come to Laramie. He's got to help us."

Father Elet didn't know what to say. Colonel Mitchell was a good friend and the Jesuits owed him a favor, but Father De Smet was needed in St. Louis. For the past two years he'd been stationed in the city as assistant to the Provincial and treasurer of the Province. His work was important and it took up all his time. And also—

"Do you really need him?"

"Need him! I've got to have him." The Colonel bit the end off a fresh cigar and lit it. "Nobody in all the West can talk to Indians the way he can—not even Jim Bridger. There isn't a tribe that doesn't know about him; even if they've never seen him, they like what they've heard about him.

"If he asks the mountain tribes to come to Laramie, they'll come. If he tells the chiefs that we're offering them a good treaty, they'll sign it. They know he'd never give them bad advice. I could go out there with a regiment of dragoons and they'd laugh at me, but let him turn up and say a word or two—and before you could say Jack Robinson, they'll be smoking the peace pipe and dipping their hands into the dog stew."

"What if he doesn't approve of your treaty?"

"Not a chance. It's all in the Indians' favor. There's another reason why he's got to come: we're going to draw up some tribal boundaries, and we need his maps and his knowledge of the trails."

Half an hour later Father Elet was walking slowly down the corridor to Father De Smet's room, pondering over the fix in which he found himself. He'd promised Colonel Mitchell that Father De Smet would be free to go to Laramie, but a more prudent superior would have found some excuse for refusing. It was true that the great missionary was needed in St. Louis for his business ability. But there was also a more recent, and a secret, reason why he shouldn't make a trip to the Indian country. A letter was on its way from Rome which would affect all Father De Smet's future actions. Father Elet was officially ignorant of what the letter said, but he could make a good guess at its contents. Still, had he the right to upset a work of so much importance to the United States Government, and to thousands of Indians, for the sake of an order which hadn't officially arrived? He thought not. As he entered Father De Smet's room he made up his mind to give the necessary permission.

Father De Smet sprang eagerly to his feet when Father Elet told him he was to attend the council.

"I'll be able to visit the Sioux again," he said. "They're a magnificent people, Father. I don't think they're quite ready for missions, but they will be soon with the grace of God."

Then the two friends sat down for a talk about the missions, and what more should be done for the Indians. For some time priests had been going out from the main villages among the Kalispels, Coeur d'Alènes and Flatheads—and from the Willamette Valley and Grand Prairie—to visit lesser stations among the Chaudieres, Okanagans, Kootenais and Flatbows. The mission to the Blackfeet was having an effect even on those hard, cruel fighters. Slowly but surely the tribes were learning to be strong and self-reliant in a white man's world. True, there had been some difficulties of late at St. Mary's, but it was nothing that a visit and a talk couldn't mend.

After Father Elet left him, Father De Smet turned to his work in a happy mood. Now that he had the Laramie council to look forward to, the daily juggle of unpaid bills and accounts receivable didn't seem so dismal. Since he'd returned from his last begging trip to Europe in 1848, he'd been virtually chained to his desk. Perhaps this new assignment meant that his superiors were ready to release him from his tour of duty as a businessman; perhaps they'd let him return for good to the missions.

He feared, sometimes, that many of his Jesuit brethren didn't understand the importance of the mountain villages. There was no actual criticism, but he sensed a mute opposition—a feeling that too much money and time were being spent in the wilderness, when there was still so much to do among so-called civilized men. If they could only see, just once, the joy and ardor of the Indians in their Faith—the patience and zeal with which they were struggling up out of savagery—he was sure they'd feel otherwise.

Chapter 6

OFF TO LARAMIE

The steamer *St Ange,* bound for Fort Union on the upper Missouri, was pushing her way through the forest and prairie country beyond the mouth of the Platte. Aboard her there was none of the usual horseplay and boisterousness of men on a voyage to the fur trapper's land. She moved like a ghost ship.

Father De Smet and Father Christian Hoecken (the brother of the Kalispels' Black Robe) had boarded the *St Ange* at St. Louis early in June. With them traveled about eighty trappers, traders and employees of the American Fur Company. There were Canadians, Swiss, Germans and Americans—the customary loud-talking, bragging and quarrelsome lot of rough characters. It had been a late spring and very rainy; the tributary streams of the Mississippi and the Missouri had swelled the rivers to flood and the waters were filled with the wreckage of houses and barns, and with countless uprooted trees.

Ten days after leaving St. Louis one of the fur company clerks fell sick. In a few hours he was dead. Cholera, most dreaded of diseases, had touched the *St. Ange.*

One after another, thirteen men died. Father Hoecken devoted himself day and night to the care of the victims. He prepared medicines, heard confessions, and anointed the dying. Father De Smet could be of no help, for a violent malarial fever had seized him and he lay half-delirious in his bunk. On June 18 he was so low that Father Hoecken promised to anoint him in the morning.

That night Father Hoecken came down with cholera. Father De Smet dragged himself to the side of his good friend and companion, heard his confession, and gave Extreme Unction to the very man who that afternoon had been hale and well. He sat beside him while he died.

When the *St. Ange* mounted the river to higher and more open country, the plague disappeared. Father De Smet grew stronger. Although his friend's death had saddened him, he had no time for morbid regrets; smallpox was ravaging the Sioux villages near the Little Medicine River. He asked the captain's permission to go ashore and went immediately to help the sick, baptizing the little children and giving their parents all the aid he could.

Next day he caught up with the *St. Ange* and continued his journey; but wherever it was possible he landed to reassure and instruct the Indians. All the villages above the great bend of the Missouri were in a panic at the news from downstream. While he was baptizing the children of the Canadians and the half-breeds, many pagans brought their little ones to him and begged that he make them also acceptable to the Master of Life.

The *St. Ange* reached Fort Union on July 14. Father De Smet worked there for two weeks, explaining the purpose of the Laramie council, answering the questions of the suspicious Indians, and instructing any who showed interest in religion. He then set out across the eight hundred miles of wilderness that lay between Fort Union and Fort Laramie. Alexander Culbertson, the superintendent of the Fur Company's trading posts on the upper Missouri, was captain of the party and it included a number of Crow, Minnetaree and Assiniboine chiefs.

It was a rough journey, but Father De Smet's big frame sat well in the saddle. They left the Yellowstone uplands on August 17 and followed the Rosebud River to its source. On the trails along the eastern base of the Big Horn Mountains they drank their fill of good water only at the crossings of the Tongue and Powder rivers. The wagon drivers swore that the mosquito-haunted sage plains and deep ravines through which they were struggling would never see them again— that is, if they were lucky enough to get out of them alive.

Because of a wrong direction given them by three Crow horse thieves whom they'd met near the Powder River, they followed a waterless valley southward and came out on the north bank of the Platte in sight of the Red Buttes. They were well westward of Laramie, close to two hundred miles out of their way.

Across the Platte River lay the Oregon Trail.

Father De Smet couldn't believe that this was the same road over which he'd first come West with the fur company's caravan. What had been a lightly marked path across the plains was now a great highway, rutted deep by the wheels of wagons in constant passage to Oregon and California. As they swung into the wearisome final stage of their journey, they passed hundreds of forsaken camp sites. Piles of litter lay everywhere—from abandoned furniture and broken wagons to the bleaching bones of horses and oxen that had perished.

"We call this the Great Medicine Road," one of the Crow chiefs said. "Many thousands of white men have gone over it to the land of the setting sun."

The priest was deeply disturbed by what he saw. The white hunger for free land and California gold had thrust this monstrous track through the ancient solitude of the plains in only ten years. What could be expected in twenty? He understood the vast restlessness of the people of the United States, but did they have to spoil everything they touched?

"The politicians call it Manifest Destiny," said Culbertson, to whom Father De Smet had voiced his thoughts. "I don't know what that means, but I do know that it's ruining the fur trade."

It was ruining much more than the fur trade. Soon the buffalo herds would be driven from the hunting grounds and wiped out. Soon the hunting grounds themselves would be claimed for homesteads, farms and pastures by the advancing whites. Knowing the Indians as he did, Father De Smet was sure that they'd fight to keep their homeland as it had always been. But what good would it do them? War would bring them only a swifter, surer ruin.

There was only one chance for them. The tribes of the plains must learn the peaceful skills of the white man, just as the mountain tribes were learning them. If they could prepare themselves to be citizens of the new states, which were destined to take the place of the wild range, they could stay on their own lands. Peaceful, thriving villages and well-tended farms would be the best argument possible to prove that they were no longer savages—that they had rights which must be respected. If they fought back, the government would have an excellent excuse for banishing them farther inland or southward. They would wind up like the eastern Indians, kenneled like animals on a tiny reservation and turning to the whisky bottle for some measure of self-respect.

More than ten thousand Indians had come in to Laramie by the first of September. Their horses and ponies had used up all the grass in the neighborhood of the fort. Thomas Fitzpatrick and Colonel Mitchell moved the place of meeting thirty-six miles down the Platte to the bottomlands at the mouth of Horse Creek. Sufficient forage would be found there.

The first meeting of the council was held on September 8. At nine in the morning a cannon was fired to signal the start of the talks. The tribes marched in from their separate camps, each singing its own special chant. They took their places in a great circle around the shelter of lodgepoles and skins which the Cheyenne women had built for the commissioners from the United States, the interpreters and the principal chiefs.

Many of the tribes present were blood enemies, but except for a short quarrel between some Sioux and Shoshones they kept absolute order. The redstone calumet or peace pipe, its three-foot stem ornamented with feathers, hair and beads, was brought out and lit by the Sioux interpreter. After Colonel Mitchell and Tom Fitzpatrick had each taken a few puffs, it was handed around the circle of chiefs.

"I bring you the words of the Great Father in Washington," began Colonel Mitchell. "He is sorry that his people have wasted so many buffalo and the grass. He will pay for the damage. But he wants the Great Medicine Road to remain open to the westward, and he wants the right to build forts along it. He fears that evil men will attack the trains of wagons unless the forts are there.

"Also, he wishes that the tribes will choose chiefs who can bring the words of each nation to him. They will tell him how much land is claimed by each tribe, and boundaries will be drawn on a piece of paper so that each will know his own place. If you do this, there need be no more fighting. The Great Father will give you $50,000 if you agree to these things—and the same amount each year thereafter, provided you keep the treaty."

The interpreters read out the terms of the treaty over and over again until the chiefs agreed that they understood what was proposed. Then each chief went off to his own band to explain what had been said and ask for advice.

Because of the wrong directions they'd received, Father De Smet and the men from the upper Missouri didn't arrive at the council until September 11, but Colonel Mitchell told them all that had taken place. The Indians were still discussing the treaty. They were pleased to see Father De Smet and he was welcome at every campfire. He soon saw that the Indians needed few arguments from him in favor of the terms offered by the United States.

"This is a good earth," Cut Nose, a chief of the Arapahos, said to him. "I thank the Great Spirit for putting me on it. If there is to be no more fighting, I am glad. I shall go home and sleep well because I shall not have to watch my horses every night, or fear for the squaws and the little children. I cannot understand why the whites do not pick out one good place and stay on it, but if they must come through our country it is fair they should pay for what they take and spoil."

Next day the chiefs returned to the council. The talks over the boundaries of tribal lands began. A large map, based on the information given by Fitzpatrick, Father De Smet and others, was prepared and each chief marked his claims down on it. There were few disputes.

Meanwhile, Father De Smet said Mass each morning and visited all the camps, preaching to the Indians and giving them religious instruction. When they asked him what he thought of the treaty, or questioned him about the white men, he told them the truth whether it pleased them or not.

"The white man is very strong," he told them. "You can win battles from him but you are sure to lose a war. If you can make peace with him on fair terms, do so. Learn his ways and practice them, when they are good."

The treaty was ready for signature by September 17. Already the Indians were "covering the dead"—the ceremony in which tribes, or bands within tribes, atoned for the death of enemy warriors by giving presents to the relatives of the slain. Sentence by sentence, the interpreters read the treaty aloud in many Indian tongues. Then the chiefs signed it and the commissioners signed it. A long-awaited wagon train of gifts—knives, clothing, tools and arms for hunting—arrived and the first installment due under the treaty was paid. Each chief received a share for his people, and the white men marveled at the justice with which the shares were split up among the tribesmen.

Soon the villages began to pack up and ride away home. Cheyenne and Aricara, Sioux and Shoshone, Crow and Arapaho—men who would have flown at one another's throats only a week or two before—all departed in peace.

Please God it will last, thought Father De Smet as he watched them go. Now many zealous priests must be found to teach these great children the arts of peace as well as the way of salvation.

Father De Smet returned to St. Louis across Kansas. Tom Fitzpatrick was taking an Indian delegation that way, to show them how well some of the eastern Indians were doing as stock raisers and farmers. For the first time the plains Indians tasted apples, peaches and melons, squash, carrots and potatoes—all raised by men like themselves. Eagle Head, who represented the Arapahos, confessed to Father De Smet that he hadn't believed it possible.

"I understand you now, Father," he said. "You told us in camp that the buffalo would last only a few years longer, but that the earth would give us food for ourselves and our children. My ears were closed when you spoke. Today I have eaten what the earth can give us and my ears are open. I see here a people who are well fed, well clothed and happy. Send us a Black Robe. We shall listen to his words."

The missionary's hopes were high as the steamboat *Clara* came up to the landing at St. Louis, but they were soon to be blasted. There was never to be any second Paraguay in the western mountains.

Father Elet had died. There was a new Father Provincial and he had received the expected letter from Rome. In the letter the General of the Jesuits forbade the opening of any more missions either in the Oregon country or on the plains. Father De Smet was ordered to confine himself to his work as treasurer and assistant to the Provincial; all the missions from now on were to be directed by the General himself.

The following reports had come to him, the General went on: that Father De Smet had exaggerated the abilities of the Indians and their readiness to be Christians; that he had made them promises which he was unable to keep; that he had encouraged them to expect too much from the missionaries.

Since the Flathead mission, supposedly the best of all, had failed miserably, he was ordering Father Mengarini to close down St. Mary's and leave the place. Enough time and money had been wasted.

Who could have reported such things? The priest stared down at the letter as if the bit of paper could answer his bewildered question. Every report from Bishop Blanchet, every word he'd heard from the men at the missions, had said just the opposite.

It was true that there had been trouble at St. Mary's, but that tragic event had been caused by a crew of drunken American traders who had tried to use the mission as a winter hotel. When they'd been ordered out, they'd avenged themselves by selling whisky to the Flatheads and by telling them that farm work would make women out of them. The simple Indians had been only too easily persuaded. Victor, their new chief, had not been strong enough to keep them all in order and many had returned to the old wandering life.

But what were missionaries for, if not to help those who fell by the wayside? Nothing had happened that couldn't be remedied. And what of the missions among the Coeur d'Alènes and the Kalispels which were flourishing in every way? And what of the success in western Oregon?

Father Provincial tried to console Father De Smet. Rome was far away, he said, and the General had to be prudent. If the criticism was shortsighted and mistaken, it would answer itself in time. And perhaps he *had* been planning on too great a scale.

Deeply discouraged by the charges, Father De Smet refused to let himself become bitter or resentful. If it were God's will that Pierre Jean De Smet should serve Him by counting pennies and keeping accounts, then he'd do so cheerfully and loyally. But his dreams and his prayers could be for the Indians and the missions. If he couldn't serve on them, he could beg for them. No one had forbidden that.

Chapter 7

New Wars and Fresh Promises

During the next six years, Father De Smet followed his new orders with obedience and zeal. If he felt that any injustice had been done him, no one ever heard of it from him. He journeyed through France, Holland and Belgium in 1853 and again in 1856—a cheerful beggar for funds to support the work of the Missouri Province of the Jesuits. His modest manner, as well as his wonderful tales of adventure in the wilderness, won him the affection and support of many Europeans. At home in St. Louis he worked hard at the business affairs of the Province.

His missionary spirit was as high as ever although it had little scope. When the "Know-Nothings"—a secret political society which opposed Catholics, particularly immigrant Catholics, by terror and violence—grew powerful, he helped his fellow Jesuits in their fight against that menace. His quick sympathy went out to all immigrants. Whenever he could get away from his desk, he was down at the levee to meet the boats coming up the Mississippi from New Orleans. The lower decks of the river boats were jammed with immigrant families, housed like animals in the narrow space behind the boilers. Father De Smet shielded them against swindlers and rascally land agents, advised them where they should settle, cared for those who were sick, and found homes for children whose parents had died on the voyage.

His fame continued to grow. Government officials came to him very often for advice about dealing with the Indians. Old friends at the western trading posts and forts wrote to him constantly. Men and women with spiritual problems sought his counsel. And the Father General of the Jesuits, after long study of the charges that had been made against Father De Smet's management of the mountain missions, decided that they were exaggerated and untrue.

However, this didn't mean that he was free to resume his missionary work among the Indians. His ability as treasurer and man of business for the Province now stood in the way. Although few boats came down the Missouri without a message for him from one or another of the tribes, reminding him that he'd promised to return to them, he saw little chance of escaping the slavery of his desk in St. Louis.

His recall to the missions, when it did come, came in a most unexpected way. In the fall of 1846, while he'd been making his way back over the prairies to St. Louis, Father De Smet had come upon a great camp of white men, women and children near Council Bluffs on the Missouri River. These people were the Mormons. They were fleeing westward from persecution, for their peculiar religious beliefs had aroused their neighbors against them. Brigham Young, their leader, had asked Father De Smet a thousand questions about the Far West. He proposed to settle there with his followers, and he needed a knowledge of the routes mapped out by the priest-explorer.

By 1856 the Mormon settlements in Utah had grown prosperous under Brigham Young's able direction. When the United States sent men from Washington to rule the territory in Young's place, the Mormons rose in armed revolt.

A military force accompanied a newly appointed governor to Utah in the fall of 1857, but the Mormon militia got the better of the soldiers and cut them off from their base of supplies.

General W. S. Harney was ordered to lead a second expedition against the Mormons in the spring of 1858. He was to rescue the first army and compel the rebels to obey the laws of the United States. Because so many of the soldiers in his command were Catholics, he asked for a chaplain and suggested that the best man whom the President could appoint would be Father De Smet. The priest was allowed to accept the appointment and to his great joy was given permission to visit the Indian missions if he found time to travel north from Utah.

The little army marched from Fort Leavenworth on the first of June, setting its route up the Blue River and then striking off across the high prairies to take the Oregon Trail at Fort Kearny.

Each morning Father De Smet celebrated his morning Mass and he was happy that many of the soldiers came to receive Holy Communion. His tent was always open to the men for friendly discussions and the soldiers became as attached to him as had the Indians. But the trail itself filled him with sad thoughts. The wagon tracks were deeper than they'd been in 1851. And from what he heard at Fort Kearny and elsewhere he realized that the good work of the Laramie treaty had been undone. The payments to the Indians were often late, and sometimes less than was due to them. There had been several raids on emigrant trains, and the government had made at least one stupid reprisal against the Indians.

Near Cottonwood Springs, he watched a Sioux warrior ride down to stare at an abandoned camp site. A pack of cards lay scattered there, a broken shaving mug and a coffeepot without a bottom. The priest could guess what the Indian was thinking: just as these common objects had been broken and discarded, so would the white man break and destroy the people of the plains. They were no longer any use to him and they stood in his way.

About five hundred miles out on the trail a courier rode up with an order from army headquarters. The Mormons had surrendered. They had agreed to accept their new governor. The troops must return at once to Fort Leavenworth.

Happy that blood had not been shed, Father De Smet accompanied General Harney back to St. Louis. He was prepared to resign his chaplaincy and return to the humdrum of everyday duty, but a mission of the greatest difficulty and importance—and far more to his own taste—was awaiting him.

Just as Father De Smet had feared, the men who first represented white civilization in the country of the missions were the scum and refuse of the frontier. White settlers in the new territories of Oregon and Washington had been spreading out over the land, seizing on the best located and most fertile sites without any regard for the rights of the Indians who dwelt on them. Gold hunters had invaded the valley of the Columbia River, bringing with them whisky and all kinds of vice.

"We took the religion of the whites because we thought it would make us better men," a Coeur d'Alene complained to one of the Jesuit missionaries. "But the whites we see are worse than we are." The tribesmen began to drift away from all the mission villages which had been built with so much labor and devotion. "You priests are white like the Americans," sneered the chief of the Yakima tribe. "You all have one heart."

In the fall of 1855, the Indians struck back. Under Kamiakin, the Yakima chief, the tribes along the lower Columbia River had begun a campaign against their white oppressors. For three years a little war had been going on between the Indians and the local militia, principally in the Yakima country and in the Walla Walla Valley. Now, in 1858, there was grave danger that all the Northwest tribes would combine against the whites. When a small body of cavalry under Colonel Edward Steptoe came near Fort Colville on a scout, the Coeur d'Alènes set upon them and routed them.

The United States Government, fearful that this success would set the whole territory ablaze, ordered General Harney to leave for Oregon at once and suppress the revolt. The order was waiting for him at St. Louis when he returned from the Mormon expedition. As soon as he'd read it, he asked Father De Smet to accompany him.

The priest needed little urging. His heart was heavy for his misguided converts, for he knew only too well how they must have resented the arrogance and greed of the white intruders. But a war would not help them. They had no idea of the crushing power the United States could bring against them. His plan for their slow education into equality with the whites had been upset by the too-swift march of white settlement, but he might still be able to save something from the wreck.

He thought of the first days at St. Mary's—of old friends, now gone, such as Ignatius the Iroquois and Big Face, the chief who had lived and died like a saint—and of that Christmas among the Kalispels fourteen years before. Men such as those were worth saving. The missions had flourished once and they would flourish again, if the just complaints of the

Indians were met with reason and honesty instead of bullets and sabers.

The mail steamer from San Francisco crossed the bar at the mouth of the Columbia River on October 23, 1858, without any of the difficulty that had beset the *Infatigable*. It was the end of a long, difficult journey for General Harney, Father De Smet and the officers of the General's staff. They had come by what was then the quickest way between St. Louis and Oregon—by railroad to New York, by ship to the Isthmus of Panama, by rail across the Isthmus to Panama City, by ship to San Francisco, and by mail packet north to Oregon.

A handsome new lighthouse sent out its beacon from Cape Disappointment and there were many other signs of change to be seen as the vessel steamed up to Fort Vancouver. Villages and town sites dotted the banks of the river as far as Astoria. Then came a stretch of forest, and then more settlements—Cathlamet, Oak Point, Rainier, St. Helen's.

Good news was waiting at the fort. While the General and his staff were at sea, Colonel George Wright had ended the military part of the revolt with one battle. His skillful handling of his small force convinced the Indians that their defeat of Colonel Steptoe had been a fluke. The restless chiefs who had stirred up the trouble were cowed by Colonel Wright's severity, but the great mass of their warriors were impressed by his humanity and tact after their defeat. They admitted that he had been just. Their loss of men in the battle was a proper vengeance for Steptoe's dead troopers—no more, no less.

General Harney knew that the peace would last only as long as the soldiers were in the field. The true cause of the rebellion—the theft of Indian lands by the whites—had not been settled or even discussed. So he asked Father De Smet to go out among the tribes and make them understand that the army wanted to be their friend. Their legal right to their lands was guaranteed by treaties; the government must recognize this and protect them. But as long as they took the law into their own hands and raided the settlements of the whites, the intruders would have a perfect excuse for dodging the main issue and denouncing the Indians as a savage menace.

Father De Smet's first act, on his way to the mountains, was to stop at Fort Walla Walla and persuade the commanding officer there to release several Spokan and Coeur d'Alene families whom he was holding as hostages. Their safe return to their own people would be a strong proof that the government meant to do right by the tribes. The officer agreed that this made sense, and the Indians went off in company with the priest, "happy as souls escaping from limbo."

They reached Sacred Heart Mission in the afternoon of November 21. It was snowing and cold, but the gratitude of the Coeur d'Alènes for the return of their brothers was warm enough to make up for the weather. Father Gazzoli and the other Jesuits at the mission were greatly relieved to hear that the United States wouldn't punish the tribe for its share in the recent outbreak.

With great pride they showed Father De Smet the new church—ninety feet long and thirty-five feet wide. It was ornamented with paintings sent from Europe and with statues of the saints which Father Ravalli had carved in wood. The village storehouses and barns were large and well made; there was a gristmill; and the Indians were learning trades in the smithy and the carpenter's shop. Some families dwelt in wooden cabins, others in bark huts, and yet others in skin lodges—each according to its own taste. The fields were in good order; each acre had returned between 80 and 120 bushels of wheat at the last harvest.

Father De Smet spent almost three months in the mountains, helping the missionaries with their work of instructing converts and preparing others to receive their First Communion. He also explained the intentions of the government to the Coeur d'Alènes and their neighbors and did his best to make them understand that peace was the best policy for red man and white man.

About the middle of February he went to St. Ignatius Mission, where Father Adrian Hoecken and more than two thousand Kalispels gave him a royal reception. The Kalispels had few contacts with white men and their mission was the most prosperous of all; some Nez Percés and Spokans had come to live there, two camps of Pend d'Oreilles and even a few Blackfeet. Soon after his arrival at St. Ignatius, many Kootenais came miles across the snow to shake his hand and assure him that they'd been faithful to all he'd taught them.

"On the eighteenth of March," he wrote later, "I crossed deep snows to St. Mary's to visit my first spiritual children, the poor and abandoned Flatheads." The ruin of such a promising beginning saddened him when he saw it, but there was some comfort in the words of the Flathead chiefs. They continued to call the people together for prayers, they told him, and they kept Sunday as God's own day. Gambling and whisky were the curses of the tribe, but if the Black Robes would come back the people could be won away from evil.

That May, when Father De Smet returned to Fort Vancouver, he brought with him a delegation of nine chiefs. These Indians had been chosen by the mountain tribes and others to explain their troubles to General Harney, and to renew, if possible, their former treaties with the United

States. Kamiakin, chief of the Yakimas, refused to join the council at the last moment. He was suspicious of the white men and did not believe their promise that he might enter the fort without risk.

The remaining chiefs sat down with General Harney and the Superintendent of Indian Affairs in a very friendly spirit. The white men told the chiefs that no Indian had anything to fear from white justice for his part in the uprising. They would leave it up to the tribes to punish their brothers who had robbed and murdered anyone who was not in arms.

The chiefs agreed to this. They said that they saw now the foolishness of war with the whites. But how else were they to prevent whites from settling on Indian land? In future, they would let any white traveler go across their country in safety; but they expected the United States to keep its promises and protect them against white settlers. If the government would make the white people stay where they belonged, there would be no more war.

General Harney and the Superintendent assured them that the government would stop all further white trespassing, provided the tribes put down the hatchet. And the two officials sent to Washington a plan which Father De Smet had drawn up and to which the Indians agreed.

It was a very fair plan. The tribes of Oregon and Washington territories were to be guaranteed a "reserve" of land on which they could support themselves by hunting and fishing while they were being taught the crafts of civilized life. This reserve would include the country around the upper course of Clark's Fork of the Columbia River, the upper valleys of the Beaver Head, the Bitterroot valley, and that part of the Kootenai country which lay south of the Canadian border. The rivers, forests and prairies of this reserve sheltered more than enough fish and game to take care of all the Indians. No white man was to set his foot in it.

Had this plan been accepted and carried out, the trouble in the Northwest would have been brought to a just and humane conclusion. But the plan was shuffled from desk to desk in Washington, and nothing ever came of it.

However, neither Father De Smet nor General Harney could read the future. When the priest left Fort Vancouver for his overland journey back to St. Louis, all seemed well. He was happy as he made his way from mission to mission until he reached Fort Benton on the Missouri—a new name for an old place. When he'd been there in 1846, it had been called Fort Lewis.

Father Congiato, who was the official Superior of the mountain missions, kept him company for a part of the way and promised that he'd reopen the missions at Fort Colville and St. Mary's. He thought, too, that Father Hoecken could be assigned to the work among the Blackfeet which Father Point had begun so long ago.

By skiff and steamboat, the weary but contented missionary descended the Missouri River. Perhaps, after so many disappointments and trials, the dream of a second Paraguay might yet come true! According to his old custom, he stopped for a day or two at various camps along the way and visited thousands of Indians—Crows, Assiniboines, Minnetarees and Sioux—preaching to them and baptizing their little children. Only one thing bothered him. The complaints about the government's failure to keep the Laramie treaty were endless, and the mighty Sioux were not likely to be patient in affliction.

Chapter 8

THE SIOUX STRIKE BACK

"Within fifteen months of Father De Smet's return to St. Louis, the United States was engaged in the saddest of all its wars—the War between the States. Missouri was a border state, half-Northern in its sympathies and half-Southern. It soon became a battleground for guerrillas. Evil men on both sides plundered and murdered in the name of patriotism.

The war changed many things in the United States. Free travel on the Mississippi and Missouri rivers was stopped; newspapers were forbidden to print the truth; men were thrown into jail on mere suspicion of treason and without trial. The Union government was desperate for want of money; there was not enough to pay for the vast expense of the war, much less to give the Indian tribes the yearly grants which were promised them by treaties.

Father De Smet was troubled deeply by all these worries, and then came a final act of oppression which forced him into action. Clergymen of all faiths were drafted into the army. The Jesuits had already supplied more than their share of chaplains. What would happen to the work of the Society if those who remained were swept from their posts by the draft?

There was nothing to do but to make an appeal to the President. When Father De Smet arrived in wartime

Washington, he was received with sympathy by Abraham Lincoln. The President listened intently while the priest poured forth his story on the woes of the Indians. Because of epidemics of disease that had swept their reservations, the Indians had been unable to plant their crops. They were eating seed corn to hold off starvation. Father De Smet reminded the President of the many broken promises made by the government; and of the injustice with which the tribes had been driven from their native places on to lands which were always strange and often barren as well. He warned Lincoln that if the tribes revolted—and they were already threatening to do this unless they received the money which had been promised them—they would join the Confederates.

The President assured the eager priest that he would do what he could. Despite the poverty of the Federal Treasury, he was as good as his word. When Father De Smet left the capital for home, he had a check in his pocket for the Osage and Potawatomi agencies. Also, he'd been assured that Jesuit priests and brothers wouldn't be expected to report if their names came up in the draft.

The war had impoverished the Missouri Jesuits. Father De Smet was hard put to it to make ends meet, but somehow he managed to keep the missions supplied. In the summer of 1862 he loaded plows, spades and other tools aboard a river boat and delivered them at Fort Benton. The long journey was like a holiday for him. At every fort and trading post where the *Spread Eagle* put in, Indians ran to meet him. Seldom had he been busier baptizing, performing marriages—and listening.

What he heard was far from pleasant. Never before had the red men spoken so bitterly about the whites. The Sioux had clearly reached the end of their patience. To the tribes of that great nation—Brules, Yanktons and Santees, Oglalas, Miniconjous and others—the settlements that were springing up along the lengthening stagecoach lines were nests of trespassers on their hunting grounds. The railway spurs reaching westward from the Mississippi River made them fear for their hills and prairies.

Treaties meant nothing to white men, they said. Every government agent was a thief and a liar. While the whites were killing one another off in the Civil War, they meant to strike for their liberties. The chance might never come again.

Father De Smet had planned to start a mission among the Sioux the following year, but nothing could be done while the tribes were in such a mood. Early in May, however, he set off for Fort Benton again, taking with him two Jesuit lay brothers who had volunteered for the mission to the Blackfeet, and some three thousand dollars worth of supplies.

Everyone told him that the steamer *Nellie Rogers* hadn't a chance of getting through to the fort. The Sioux war, long threatening, had broken out. The Santees, under their chief Little Crow, had already run wild against the frontier settlements in Minnesota, killing many whites before the United States soldiers drove them westward into the Dakotas. By now, there were war parties out along the Platte and the Missouri. And there would be danger even before the steamer reached the plains. Confederate guerrillas were active along the Missouri River's lower course.

In spite of these dismal warnings, the *Nellie Rogers* ran into no serious trouble until she was about three hundred miles eastward of Fort Benton. It had been a very dry spring. Now in June, the thermometer stood at 100 degrees; the wind blew constant and hot. All the little streams had dried up. The Missouri itself was so low that the steamboat couldn't get beyond the mouth of the Milk River. The freight and the passengers were landed near a little fringe of woods to wait until an ox train could be sent for them from the fort.

The passengers camped among the trees and made the best of their plight. Father De Smet and the two Jesuit brothers set up their tent in the shade of some big cottonwoods. Many peaceful Crows and Gros Ventres came to visit them, but on the morning of July 4 another kind of visitor called. A shower of arrows fell into camp, wounding two of the white men. Looking up at the ridge above the camp, they saw a war party of more than six hundred Sioux waiting to descend on them.

The white men snatched up their guns and made ready to sell their lives dearly, but Father De Smet spared them the trouble. He walked out alone from the shelter of the trees and made the sign of friendship to some Sioux scouts who had ridden up close. The nearest scout recognized him and shouted his name to the others.

The Indians waited uncertainly for a moment—then one of them rode forward, shouting: "This is the Black Robe who saved my sister!" Father De Smet took the brave's outstretched hand. Beneath the warrior's paint was the face of a son of Red Fish, head chief of the Oglalas. Fifteen years before, Red Fish's daughter had been taken captive by the Crows and Father De Smet had been responsible for her safe return.

The Sioux had not forgotten this act of kindness, and now the scouts signaled to the waiting warriors to call off their attack. The priest and the scouts sat down for a friendly talk. After listening to their many complaints against the whites, Father De Smet made them a present of coffee, sugar and biscuits. The Indians thanked him, he blessed them, and they rode off.

There were no further alarms during the four weeks they sat under the cottonwoods, waiting for the ox train. When it finally arrived, the stranded travelers loaded their gear into the carts and set off again for Fort Benton. Each night they made camp beside waterholes which were mere pools of bitter-tasting mud. By day the heat was torrid. The animals suffered from want of grass. But they reached the fort at last and Father De Smet presented the two lay brothers to Father Imoda who had journeyed from the Blackfeet mission to meet them.

The Black Robe had intended to return the way he came, but the temper of the Indians made this impossible. Everyone warned him against descending the Missouri. There was water enough only for skiffs, and travel in a small, open boat would be suicide. Although many Sioux knew and respected him, the chances were even that he'd come upon a band to whom he was only another hated white man. His safest course would be a trip over the mountains to the coast of Oregon, where he could take passage aboard a ship and return to the east coast by sea. This seemed like good advice, so he set off for Fort Vancouver.

He heard some grim news as he journeyed from mission to mission. The villages were all in good condition, even St. Mary's which Father Ravalli was rebuilding; but gold had been discovered in Montana. The first strikes had been made at a spot quite close to the mission country. Already, the whites were complaining to the government about the lands under cultivation by the Indians and were reaching out greedy hands to seize them. How soon would it be before they brushed the mountain Indians off their last holdings and dispersed them into the arid, worthless hill country?

Father De Smet sailed from Portland, Oregon, on October 13. After a brief stop in Washington City, he arrived home in St. Louis on the first day of December. The trip had been long, trying and disappointing. His now dearest wish—to begin a permanent mission among the Sioux—seemed farther off than ever. And Father De Smet realized that he was getting old. His rheumatic pains were constant; he had violent headaches; somehow he always felt tired. He spent a good part of the winter confined to his room or to the house, but his gay and kindly nature was unaffected by his illness. When friends sympathized with him, he quoted an old Flemish proverb: "Though the legs creak, the heart's good."

At Washington, Father De Smet had seen the Secretary of the Interior and the Commissioner of Indian Affairs. They'd had enough of war with the Sioux, with whom the Cheyennes and Arapahos had recently joined as allies. The United States had spent twenty million dollars during 1862 and 1863 on military action against the hostile tribes. General Sibley had defeated them in several skirmishes; thirty-eight Sioux prisoners had been hanged for their share in the Minnesota massacres; but there was no sign of the rebel tribes giving in. They were too wise to stand and face the soldiers in formal battle. When they were attacked, they retreated into the badlands where the soldiers couldn't follow them.

The Secretary and the Commissioner had proposed to Father De Smet that he accompany General Alfred Sully on a new expedition against the hostile bands. While the General overawed the Indians with his troops, Father De Smet was supposed to offer them the government's new terms of peace.

The wise and experienced Black Robe thought he had never heard anything so foolish. As politely as he could, he explained to the gentlemen that the Sioux might take a different view of the matter. War was war to the Indians; peace was peace. A peacemaker could never go to the Sioux in the company of soldiers, least of all a Black Robe peacemaker. The best way to pass along the offers of the government would be by way of those bands of Sioux who disapproved of the war and had kept peace with the whites. Through the neutral tribesmen, he could reach their brothers in revolt and he would be happy to make the attempt.

To this the Secretary was pleased to agree, and Father De Smet set off once again to the upper Missouri country. Many of his friends were sure that he was heading for certain death. The Sioux had sworn that they would let no boat pass through. Yet on June 9, 1864, he reached the old Mandan trading post, now called Fort Berthold, and sent out word to the hostiles that he was ready to talk peace. The Yankton band, who had remained neutral, were encamped near the fort and some of them carried his message out on the plains.

A month later, the answer came—a war party, three hundred strong, which set up camp on the opposite bank of the Missouri and scared the whites at the fort almost out of their skins.

The Black Robe was not afraid. Calmly, he crossed the river and sat down in council with the chiefs. They had come to talk to him, they said, because they trusted him. And if the United States would send men who could be trusted, the Sioux were all willing to talk peace. The government could prove its good faith, they said, by punishing the Indian agents who had grown rich by swindling the tribes in their charge. Even the Santees, the tribe who had begun the war, were willing to talk peace. Soon after the talks at Fort Berthold, they sent a message inviting Father De Smet to their camp near the border of Canada.

Overjoyed, the priest wished to start at once for the Santee camp, but first he had to let General Sully know what was happening.

"The Indians must get a blow they'll remember," the General told him angrily. "Any tribe that harbors the murderer of a white man must be punished. They must give the murderers up to justice before we'll talk peace to them."

Father De Smet's two-hundred-mile trip to the army's advanced headquarters had been all for nothing. He tried to make the General understand that no tribe or band of Indians could possibly surrender any of their brothers to the white man's justice; it would be against all Indian laws and customs. The General remained stubborn; he had his orders and he meant to follow them out to the letter.

When Father De Smet realized that an honest peace was impossible, he returned at once to St. Louis. He could not deceive his Indian friends by offering peace terms from one department of the government which another department had no intention of honoring.

One month later General Sully defeated a united force of the Sioux at Killdeer Mountain but he didn't subdue them. The hostiles broke up into small, separate groups after the battle and hid out until they could try again. Their "punishment" only made them more determined to resist.

The Civil War dragged on. Except for yet another voyage abroad in search of money and recruits for the Society, Father De Smet continued to toil at his desk. He was far from well; an intermittent fever and sleeplessness sapped his strength, but in all his own difficulties he never forgot the troubles of the Indians. Their miseries were great. The winters of 1865 and 1866 were long and cold. Many bands of the Sioux had been forced to eat their horses. Many children had died.

Hundreds of new scalps dangled from the lances of the hostiles; the warriors had added many more eagle feathers to their bonnets in token of enemies slain. Their anger burned more fiercely than ever against the white treaty breakers. War parties were everywhere.

One day a whirlwind of red raiders would strike an emigrant train on its slow way along the Platte; the next day, a boat's crew on the Missouri would be surprised, their scalps lifted, and the cargo looted. Whenever the soldiers concentrated and moved out from the forts, the Sioux vanished like ghosts. They had no towns or forts to defend, no baggage or pack trains to worry about. Their wives, children and old people were hidden away safely in camps of which the soldiers knew nothing.

The United States Government had ordered a road to be opened to the new gold fields in Montana. It was to run northwestward from Fort Laramie and along the eastern face of the Big Horn Mountains—right across the choicest hunting grounds of the Sioux. Some of the more timid bands had given their consent for the building of the road at a council in June 1866, but the great fighting chief Red Cloud had walked out on the council. Red Cloud sent a scornful message to Colonel H. B. Carrington who commanded the troops assigned to guard the road builders:

"You are the man who came to steal the road. I will not talk to you. I will fight you. As long as I live, I will fight you for the last hunting grounds of my people."

Colonel Carrington had replied by marching the Eighteenth Infantry from Laramie to the Powder River country in the blistering heat of July. He enlarged a stockade which had been put up during the previous year and called it Fort Reno. Then he began building two more forts farther up the line of the new road—Fort Phil Kearny and Fort C. F. Smith. Red Cloud watched these operations and bided his time. His warriors sniped at the soldiers from the brushwood, raided outposts, and ambushed work parties in search of wood and water. His plan was a simple one. He would wait for the snow to fall, then he would cut off the forts from their base of supplies and starve the garrisons into surrender.

By late autumn of 1866 the Indians were keeping so close a watch on Fort Phil Kearny that Colonel Carrington forbade any man to leave it without a pass and an escort. The soldiers grew restless. Arrows fell into the fort. Each day the soldiers woke to watch the Indians moving on ceaseless patrol along the ridges. Was no one brave enough to teach the redskins a lesson? Captain Fetterman bragged that he could defeat the whole Sioux nation with only eighty men. Why did they have to stay cooped up in the fort?

A party of woodcutters marched out on December 21 under protection of a small escort. They'd barely reached the wooded hills when they signaled that they were being attacked. Captain Fetterman rushed out to their rescue with some soldiers—just eighty of them, as it happened. Foolishly, he took no precautions and made no scout. As he pursued what he thought were a few fleeing Indians over Lodge Trail ridge, the main Sioux force rose up out of the ravines on the far side. Every soldier was slain.

The news of Red Cloud's little victory ran like wildfire through all the Sioux country and filled the Indians with hope and new courage. Many of the bands decreed a sort of martial law and the war chiefs took over with full authority. Even the bands that were supposed to be neutral and opposed to the war could no longer be trusted. At any time some eloquent fighting chief might talk their young men into riding off to join the hostiles.

When the news of the Fetterman massacre reached Washington, the president ordered that no further attempt to "punish" the Sioux should be made until the tribes had been offered a fair and honest treaty of peace. And that was why, after neglecting him for three years, the Secretary of the Interior called on Father De Smet for help.

"I'll be on the road within a week," the priest wrote to his brother Francis, on March 29, 1867. "The Secretary requests me to go to the hostile Indians—to try to bring them back to peace and submission, and to prevent as much as possible the destruction of property and the murder of the whites."

It was high time, he thought as he signed the letter, blotted it and sealed it. He was not sure he'd succeed. The hostile bands had been willing to talk to him in 1864, but in their present mood they were just as likely to regard him as only another white enemy—to be killed on sight. His best chance would be to make contact with the hostiles through the Yankton group of the Sioux. They were at peace with the government and were living on a reservation near Fort Randall. Their chief, Man-Who-Strikes-the-Ree, was his old friend and convert.

Man-Who-Strikes-the-Ree and a group of Yankton warriors rode with him when he started up the Missouri from Fort Randall at the end of April. They journeyed from camp to camp all the way to Fort Pierre; at each stop Father De Smet urged the Indians to be patient. The bad treatment they'd received had aroused even the most peaceful tribes, but he promised them that the Great Father in Washington was at last coming to their aid. One large band of hostiles to whom he talked told him that they were quite willing to settle on a reservation and become farmers if the Great Father wished it—but until the promised reservation with its fields and stables and animals and schools was actually theirs, they must continue to range as they pleased. How would they eat, if they couldn't move about after game?

At Fort Pierre he met General Alfred Sully and General E. S. Parker. General Sully had learned wisdom through experience. He was no longer anxious to "punish" the Sioux.

"Our orders from Washington say that we must hear every Indian complaint," he told Father De Smet. "We're supposed to root out every crooked agent and report on every trespassing settler. If they'd given me such orders in 1864," he went on, "we'd have been spared a lot of trouble."

At the generals' request, the priest took them along with him as far as the junction of the Missouri and the Yellowstone rivers. Word had gone out among the Indians that the Black Robe was coming, and at each fort and trading post were many Sioux, Assiniboines and Crows, waiting to hear what he had to say. Father De Smet introduced the generals to each group of Indians, explained that they'd come to learn what the Indians wanted, and called on the Indians to speak their minds.

The complaints were many. When the corn crop of one tribe had failed, and the Indian mothers came with their starving babies to look for food in the garbage heap at Fort Berthold, the commander there had ordered scalding water to be thrown on them. But the complaints of the tribesmen were not so much against individuals as against the whole policy of the United States. Iron Shield, chief of the Minicon jous, summed them up:

"When the Great Father," he began, "sends honest men to my country I am glad to speak with them. Among you is one known to me, a man of God: I and my people love him. You tell me that the Great Father loves his redskinned children, that he wishes to be just to them and make them happy. Formerly we were happy, because the whites who came to us to hold council did not deceive the Indians. If the Great Father really loves us, why has he sent agents into our country who lie to us? Since the coming of these men all is changed, prosperity and goodness have disappeared.

"We have never troubled your lands, and you come to ours to sow unhappiness. Why do you do this? You have built four railroads through our country and driven away the wild animals. You refuse us powder and bullets, and why? The game has become so shy that my bow and arrow are useless. I now need powder and lead.

"Since the white man has come here and deceived us we cannot live in contact with him. I am ashamed to put my foot in a white man's lodge or to receive him in mine. Also, the soldiers have treated us badly. If the Great Father would recall them and leave us only the traders whom we need, happiness would return.

"This is my country; it does not belong to you, and we have no intention of surrendering it. We do not wish to inhabit the lands you offer; we wish to live here, and I and my warriors choose rather to fight and die in defending our rights rather than leave our country and die of starvation. Moreover, we swear to scalp every white man that falls into our hands, if the Great Father does not withdraw the soldiers and restore to us our lands. I have spoken."

Father De Smet didn't wonder at the bitterness and anger of the Indians. Yet war would do them no good. By August, the red man's faith in the Black Robe expressed itself in the promise of fifteen thousand Indians to keep the peace until a new treaty could be offered them. This success encouraged Father De Smet to consider striking out into the interior in search of other hostile bands. But at this point his strength failed him. He had worked so hard during the past months as peacemaker and missionary that he could go on no longer. He returned to St. Louis, ill and weary, comforted only by the knowledge that to the Indians he was "the white man whose tongue does not lie."

Chapter 9

IN THE CAMP OF SITTING BULL

All that winter, while Father De Smet was recovering his strength, a new commission was working to settle the Sioux wars for good. The President had appointed Generals Terry, Sheridan, and Sherman, as well as Father De Smet's old friend, General Harney, to study the evidence and draw up treaty terms.

The Commissioners invited Father De Smet to work with them, and, while he could not join their meetings, he was satisfied with their decisions. The Sioux would fare well under the new treaty. Moreover, since in future the agencies would be governed by army officers, the tribes would no longer have to fear the dishonesty of the political agents.

By March Father De Smet had made up his mind, tired and ailing though he was, to set out for the Sioux country. The Commissioners had called a great council of all the tribes to meet at three places: the forks of the Platte River, Fort Laramie, and Fort Rice. The priest wanted to be present at the meetings to help assure the Indians of the wisdom of the treaty. But when he and the Commissioners arrived at the forks, only one group of Sioux was awaiting them there. What was worse, the Hunkpapas, Oglalas and Miniconjous— the most powerful members of the Sioux nation—sent word that they wanted nothing to do with the Commissioners or their treaty.

When the generals heard this bad news they were ready to throw up their hands and abandon their mission. Father De Smet urged them not to give up so easily. The treaty was a good one; the Sioux must be persuaded to hear its terms at least.

"If only someone would go to the hostiles and convince them that the government means business," he told the generals, "I'm sure they'd come in. They've been tricked so often in the past that they're suspicious."

"But they've warned every white man out of their country—even the traders who've dealt with them for years. It would be suicide for anyone to seek them out where they're hiding. And we don't even know where they are."

"I can find them," said the priest confidently. It was true. The neutral Sioux wouldn't have betrayed the hiding place of their brothers to a white soldier, even under torture—but Father De Smet had only to ask and they'd tell him.

"You're an old man—you're sixty-eight years old, and your health isn't good."

"So much the better," he answered, smiling. "My white scalp wouldn't be much of a trophy. I'm not afraid to go—so why are you afraid for me?"

The Commissioners argued with him for a long time. The hostiles had threatened *every* white man, they said. And if he sent a message to the chiefs, asking for permission to come, the summer would be gone before an answer could be received. Father De Smet replied that he'd merely send word of his coming, and go. God would take care of him. His black robe and missionary cross were symbols of peace and the Indians knew it.

"You're the only man in the whole United States who has even a chance of succeeding," General Harney admitted.

"Ten years ago, I'd have said you couldn't fail—even five years ago! But in the present temper of the hostiles, I feel as if I'm letting you go to your death."

"We're both soldiers," said the priest, "even though I wear a different uniform. You'd go if you could see any chance of success, because you'd feel it your duty. Well, it's my duty, too, and I can succeed. Therefore, I should go. A simple demonstration of logic, gentlemen."

The steamer *Columbia* nosed into the landing at Fort Rice on May 24. Father De Smet was pretty sure that the great camp of the hostiles was somewhere in the Yellowstone Valley—probably near the mouth of Powder River. By riding westward from Fort Rice he could pick up the trail of the Indians in the shortest possible time, and he was counting on the help of friendly Sioux who lived near the fort. They could give their fighting brothers advance warning that he proposed to visit them.

Hundreds of Indians had come in to the fort to hear what the Commissioners had to say. Father De Smet's word that the government men were coming with a good treaty pleased them greatly. But when he went on to say that he meant to journey out over the badlands in search of the hostile bands, the chiefs begged him not to go. The winter had been long and hard, they said. Their brothers had had much time to brood over their wrongs. Not even the Black Robe would be safe among them.

There could be no treaty unless the hostiles came in and signed it, he answered. As late as January, several Hunkpapa and Miniconjou chiefs had sent him messages and promised to listen to him if he came to them. That might have been so in January, replied the friendly chiefs, but if he valued his scalp, he'd better stay at Fort Rice.

"In St. Louis, and in many other places," he said calmly, "thousands of little children are praying for me and for those who go with me. I trust myself to God's hands. I will go."

Above all other virtues, the Indians prized courage. They threw up their hands in admiration and shouted applause. Many of them offered to go with him and urge their brothers to hear him.

He said Mass early on the morning of June 3 and prayed that God would protect him and his companions on their dangerous journey. Then, surrounded by the chiefs Running Antelope, Two Bears, All-Over-Black, The Log, Little Dog, Returning Ghost, Bear's Rib, and Sitting Crow, who headed his escort of eighty picked warriors, he said good-by.

"A large circle was formed," wrote Father De Smet, "in which several officers and some of the soldiers from the fort joined. I offered a solemn prayer to the Great Spirit and put us in His keeping. Our march westward began at seven in the morning. That first day we made twenty-two miles and camped on the north bank of the Cannonball River."

It was a dry season. The river was only a trickle. Thereafter, for more than three hundred miles, the peacemakers rode through a succession of broad, rolling plains and high buttes. There wasn't a tree to be seen; stunted shrubs struggled for life along the dry watercourses. The surface of the buttes was rocky and sterile and covered with bits of lava and petrified wood. The plains were rich with buffalo grass, so they didn't suffer for want of food. Deer, antelope, and buffalo were plentiful.

After six days of hard riding the party expected to come upon some traces of the hostile bands and their camp, but they found none. Could his information have been wrong, thought the priest? Could the camp have been shifted?

It would be foolish as well as dangerous to stumble on it without warning. He had to get word to the hostile chiefs that he was coming; otherwise, even if he kept his scalp, his mission would have small chance of succeeding. Indians resented even the slightest breach of courtesy.

Little Dog, Sitting Crow, and The Log offered to ride off and make a wide scout while the rest of the party continued to push westward. The scouts took a present of tobacco with them. Should they meet the hostiles and the tobacco be accepted when it was given, that would mean peace and a willingness to talk. But if the present should be refused—then they'd all better ride for Fort Rice as fast as they could.

Another week went by—the scouts did not return. The desert country shimmered in the heat. Water, when they could find any, was stagnant and green; cactus and sage were all the vegetation. The Indians of the escort grew more and more silent, and that was a bad sign.

Then, late one afternoon as they were setting up camp, one of the Indians leaped up and shouted. Far in the distance a great cloud of dust had arisen. Father De Smet felt his heart beat faster. Death might be riding toward them in that cloud. Although he'd faced danger and death many times before, he'd never been able to regard it with the calm nerves of which other explorers told in their books. He did all he could do—he whispered a prayer to Our Lady, and waited.

The dust cloud grew larger and drew nearer; within it a body of horsemen were riding furiously. The priest took a view of them through his field glass and at once relaxed. They were eighteen in number, and in the lead galloped his own three scouts.

The horsemen rode up to the camp, shouting and singing. They brought good news. The head chiefs of the hostile bands had sent them to tell the Black Robe that his present of tobacco had been received with favor. They would hear his words. He was welcome to visit their camp and smoke the calumet with Sitting Bull and the other chiefs. That night the Indians of the escort gave the strangers a great and noisy feast. Early next morning they all set off for a three-day ride over a desolate and arid plain.

On June 19, after crossing a plateau about twelve miles wide, they reached the high bluffs that bounded the valley of the Powder River. Its tree-lined course was a happy sight after so many days in the badlands. And there was something else to see! Below their station on the bluffs, about four miles down the bottoms of the river, a great troop of Indians—five hundred at least—were riding toward them at breakneck speed. Father De Smet had brought a banner with him; on one side it bore the image of the Blessed Mother, on the other was embroidered the holy name of Jesus. He raised it on high—and instantly the horsemen reined in and formed a line of battle.

A few chiefs rode forward very cautiously to make a scout. When they saw what the banner represented—and that it was not the hated flag of the United States—they shouted and shook their lances. At this signal their followers started forward again. Father De Smet's escort formed in line and rode down from the bluff; the two groups met near the river with many joyous whoops and cries. The hostiles were in all their glory of paint and eagle feathers. Their deerskin leggings and the manes of their horses were decorated with enemy scalps. Some carried lances and bows; many had guns.

The new arrivals greeted Father De Smet with great ceremony and kindness. Sitting Bull had ordered four chiefs to keep watch over the Black Robe night and day, they said, so long as he stayed in their camp. Many of the warriors had lost members of their families in battle with the soldiers, and they might think themselves obliged by Indian law to take revenge on the first white man they met. After shaking hands with every man in the reception party, Father De Smet asked if they might go at once to the camp. The Indians crossed over Powder River and formed in close column for the twelve-mile ride.

The priest had never seen a larger camp in all his travels. It held more than a thousand lodges. At its very center a roomy lodge had been prepared for his use and the principal chiefs were waiting there for him—Sitting Bull, Black Moon the orator or spokesman, No Neck, and Four Horns who was the head chief of the camp. He thanked them for their splendid reception of him and they told him that they were ready to hold a council with him in the morning. They were all very frank in expressing their feelings about the war.

"The whites began all this trouble," said Sitting Bull. "When they killed six hundred Cheyennes at Sand Creek— not warriors only, but women and children and old men— all my veins were shaken. I took up my tomahawk and have done all the harm to the whites that I could. You come at a bad time, Black Robe, but you have never lied to us. I will listen to your good words at the council."

Father De Smet met the chiefs next morning at the council ground. Around a circular space covering half an acre, the women had hung many *tipi* skins on posts. Opposite the entrance to this roofless tent they'd set up Father De Smet's banner and placed next to it a seat made of the finest buffalo robes. When all the chiefs had taken their places inside the enclosure, the priest was led to his seat of honor and the council was opened with ceremonial songs and dances. Four

Horns lighted the calumet, offered the first puffs to the Great Spirit, and handed it to Father De Smet. It passed all around the circle and each chief took a few puffs. Then the head chief said gravely, "Speak, Black Robe, my ears are open to hear your words."

The priest rose and spoke for more than an hour. He told the Indians that nothing but a wish to see them happy and at peace had brought him to their camp. The white man was very strong—strong enough to destroy the Sioux if he put forth all his strength. But the Great Father in Washington did not want to destroy them; he hoped, by treating them kindly, to make them his friends. All the crimes committed by both sides should be buried and forgotten.

The Great Father would give them cows and horses and tools for farming. He would send good, wise men who could show them how to get their food from the soil. He would send other good men to teach the Indian children the skills and arts of his own people.

Every foot of land east of the Big Horn Mountains and above the north fork of the Platte was theirs and would remain theirs—the Great Father would punish any white man who tried to settle there. Honest men were waiting at Fort Rice to promise all this and to sign a treaty in the name of the Great Father. They were famous war chiefs of the whites; their word was good.

As he was speaking, he watched the play of emotion over the dark faces—rage, shame and savage frustration lit their eyes when he spoke of their possible defeat; their hands clutched convulsively at the air; they shouted in guttural tones. No matter, he thought. Whether they liked it or not, he must tell them the truth.

When he'd finished, four chiefs rose and replied to him. What the Great Father promised was good, they said—but it wasn't enough. He must destroy the forts he'd built along the road to Montana. He must make his people treat the Indians like men—not like dogs, as they were fond of doing. Sitting Bull insisted that no more land be given to settlers, and that the whites respect the trees, in particular the oak, which the Indians could not bear to see cut down.

If the Great Father swore to do all these things, the Sioux were ready to bury all the evil done in the past. They would fight no more. A group of wise chiefs would be chosen to go to Fort Rice with the Black Robe. If the white war chiefs spoke true words, they would sign a treaty.

Black Moon thanked Father De Smet for traveling so far to help them. And then, "after singing and dancing that shook the hills and made the earth tremble," as the priest described it, the council was closed. For the rest of that day he stayed in his lodge, talking to the many Indians who visited him. He blessed a large number of children whom their mothers brought to him—grown boys and girls, toddlers, and papooses strapped to cradle boards.

On June 21 the head chiefs and many warriors escorted the priest and his Yankton friends back as far as the Powder River. Eight principal men of the Hunkpapa and Miniconjou groups took the trail eastward with him. All-Over-Black rode on ahead to tell the Commissioners that envoys from the hostile camp were coming.

Fort Rice came alive with joy at the news that Father De Smet was safe and that his mission had been a success. Soldiers and Indians streamed out to meet him, the braves draped in their mantles, feathers and ribbons decorating their heads, and red paint daubed on their faces. The warriors formed into ranks and paraded before their Black Robe, welcoming him back with cries of pleasure.

Immediately arrangements were made to hold a great peace council on July 2. More than fifty thousand Indians were represented by their warrior envoys. Solemn promises were made by both sides to observe the terms of the treaty, and then the signing took place. At last both sides felt satisfied that the Sioux wars had come to an end. Only one threat remained: Red Cloud and his Oglalas refused to honor the treaty until they saw with their own eyes the destruction of the forts along the Montana road.

The government men were loud in their praises for what the aging priest had accomplished. "Whatever may be the result of the treaty," wrote Major-General David Stanley, who had been present at the council, "we can never forget—nor shall we ever cease to admire—the disinterested devotion of

Father De Smet."

But Father De Smet was too humble to listen long to the compliments of the Commissioners. As soon as the treaty was signed, he left for St. Louis to take up again the financial burden of the Missouri Jesuits. There was peace in his heart as the steamboat edged its way down-river—a peace that was to be as short-lived as the promises that had been made to the Indians.

Chapter 10

"THE INDIANS COVERED THEIR HEADS . . ."

Spring came on slowly in the year 1873—too slowly to suit an ailing old man. A useless old man, too, thought Father De Smet, as he stared out from the window of his room at the rain falling in the street.

Since the doctor had ordered him to stay in his room, he'd completed eighty pages of a history of the Missouri Province. The manuscript lay on his desk and he should be working on it, but even writing—which he'd always enjoyed—now seemed difficult. The sight of his mantel piece, lined with pillboxes and druggists' bottles, took his appetite away.

Tomorrow his dear old friend Captain La Barge expected him to be present at the launching of a new river boat. He wished he hadn't promised to go. Yet how many men had a steamboat named after them while they were still around to see it launched? His sense of fun returned as he thought of the good ship *De Smet* bucking the Missouri River current while her crew howled wrathfully at the snags.

A knock came at the door. He called, "Come in," and a young man entered and stood waiting, smiling a little uncertainly.

"Yes, Father?"

"You said I might come and talk with you." The young man's face fell as he realized that Father De Smet had forgotten him. "But if it's too much trouble—"

"Not at all, not at all." Of course. This was the young priest from Boston who'd spoken to him a day ago, or was it two days ago? He was assigned to the Indian missions. "Sit down. I'm glad you've come. What can I do for you?"

"I shan't disturb you long," the visitor began. He didn't take the offered chair but stood, tall and troubled, nervously washing one hand against the other. "Perhaps I shouldn't have come here at all—but no one can advise me better than you. You see—"

He paused, and then went on hurriedly: "Ever since I was a boy, I've wanted to work with the Indians. I entered the Society hoping my superiors would let me go West, if it were the will of God. I've done my best—I've tried to learn the Indian languages and their customs. But now that I'm on my way to the missions, I—I'm—"

Father De Smet said nothing. Save for a gentle smile on his lips, he might have been asleep.

"I'm afraid," the young priest concluded in a low, shamed voice.

"Of what? Work, trouble, disappointment?"

"Of failure, Father. Afraid that I'm unfit—that I'll drive souls away from Christ instead of bringing them to Him. I can't make any mistakes where men's souls are concerned."

"The Indians are simple people," said Father De Smet after a long silence. "If you go to them in love and kindness, if you see in each one of them—even the worst—the image of our Saviour, you cannot fail. They'll look deep into your heart, my son, and if what they see there is good they'll listen to your words. I know no tricks to teach you—no easy means."

"But I can't be sure."

"No one can," the old man continued. "I think you're being tempted. It's a very subtle temptation—the fear of failure. A man who does nothing is never wrong in the world's eyes, but inaction produces nothing. It's only cowardice in disguise. You're young, you've a long life before you. You must be strong and confident. Go and do your best. God will help you. Pray."

When the young priest left him, Father De Smet went to the window again. The gray and rain-soaked view of the street brought him no comfort. It had been easy enough to counsel a young man against the fear of failure; it was harder to face the fact of failure in oneself. How had he found the courage to speak so confidently? Pierre Jean De Smet was a failure; no one knew it better than himself.

His life's work had come to nothing. His great plan for "reductions"—reserves of wild land on which the Indians could maintain their tribal identity and their self-respect— had never even been tried. A wiser, better man would have been able to convince the government of the idea's value and importance. After thirty-three years of effort by the priests and brothers who had labored so hard and so well, what was there to show?

Three years before, President Grant had dealt the Catholic missions a deathblow. Of forty-three Indian reservations on to which the tribes had been herded, the Catholics had been excluded by law from all but four. The new Superintendent of Indian Affairs had turned over to his Protestant friends many of the schools and churches which Indian labor and the generosity of white Catholics had raised in the wilderness. Eighty thousand Indians, baptized in the Catholic faith, had been turned into Methodists, Quakers, and Presbyterians without their consent. At the Yakima reservation, the government agent forbade the entry of any Catholic priest for any reason.

The government cared no more for the property rights of the Indians than it did for their religious rights. The year or two of comparative justice that had followed the signing of the treaty in 1868 had ended in further land grabbing by the whites. The government agents who for several years had been trying to force the Flatheads and Kalispels off their lands in the valley of the Bitterroot had won finally by fraud what law and reason had failed to get them. The signature of the Flathead chief had been forged to an agreement by which his people gave up their rights and consented to settle near Missoula, Montana.

Long since the smaller tribes of Oregon and Washington had been sent to tiny, unsuitable reservations and were lost among the conquering whites. After much talk about a permanent mission among the Sioux at Grand River, nothing had been done. His Catholic converts there, and among all the Sioux bands, were given over to missionary efforts of many sects. All letters of protest to Washington had gone unanswered.

Four small and scattered mission stations to show for a lifetime of labor! Did the fault lie in him? Had he been too ambitious, too proud—and was this the Lord's way of humbling him? Or were the greed and land hunger of white men so strong that no man's efforts could stem them?

The Indians themselves might share the blame. His critics might have been right when they'd said that he overrated the abilities of the Indians. They preferred a wandering life. They loved drink and gambling. They had little sense of responsibility for what they did. By their ancient laws and customs, honest labor was mean and unmanly. Had he been struggling upstream in his efforts to save them; had they been doomed from the start by some monstrous operation of history?

It was almost dusk. The rain had stopped but the air was heavy with fog. He turned away from the window and lit the lamp on his desk. He took down from his bookshelf a volume which had never failed to comfort him in moments of dejection—the letters of St. Francis Xavier. Slowly and with difficulty, for his bones ached, he seated himself in a chair and prepared to read.

But he held the book on his lap unopened. His mind was too uneasy for him to sit quietly and turn pages. Faces of people, long since forgotten, began to swim before his mind's eye. Some were strangers he'd met by chance on his river journeys and his voyages abroad; some were soldiers and *engagés* at the forts and trading posts, old friends, whom he'd counseled in their troubles. There were Indians beyond number in his dreaming.

He saw once more the Flatheads running to meet him when he came to Fort Hall on his second missionary journey—that was old Simon in front, running at his best speed. The others had wanted to leave the old man at the camp, but the ardor of his youth returned and he'd made the long ride with the best of them.

He saw the kindly, placid face of Louise Sighouin, dead these many years. She was a chief's daughter of the Coeur d'Alènes, but she had lived a life of poverty by choice, serving her tribe as nurse to the sick and foster mother of orphans. No work of charity had been too hard or too mean for her.

He saw that old Sioux who had come to his lodge in Sitting Bull's camp—a bowed and wrinkled figure, clutching in his hand a little copper cross. "Where did you get it?" he'd asked, and the old man answered: "From you, Black Robe, when you came to our village. And ever since, for twenty-six years, whenever I was drawn to do evil things I have taken it in my hand and thought of the goodness of the Master of Life."

He remembered the blind Chaudiere, lame and close to death, who'd been carried in to baptism by his fellow tribesmen. "My life has been long," the man had said. "For many years I've wept for my children who are gone from me, and for my friends who are gone. I live like a stranger in my tribe. Yet today the Great Spirit has taken pity on me. I offer Him my heart and my life."

The faces faded, glimmered and were gone. But memory had brought peace. What did it matter, in God's great purpose, that material things came to nothing? If even a few men and women were brought to know God, to love Him and serve Him—that was all that mattered. Farms, plans, buildings of good brick and mortar, sermons, schools—none of these could accomplish the regeneration of the Indians by itself. God would bring it about through His grace in His own way—which need not be Pierre Jean De Smet's way. He had done his work as best he could; he hoped humbly that God was pleased with his efforts. But what men thought of them—and whether they'd failed by human standards—was supremely unimportant.

Happily, he opened his book and read: "Among other intercessions, I have recourse to the children I have baptized and whom God, in His infinite mercy, called to Himself before they had stained their baptismal robes. I invoke them to obtain for me the grace to do God's will in the way He wills it upon this earth of exile and misery."

So St. Francis Xavier had written, and so prayed Father De Smet.

The old missionary died on May 23, 1873. He was buried in the Jesuit cemetery at Florissant just fifty years after he'd come there as a novice. The steamboat *De Smet* carried the news up the Missouri River on her first voyage. The Indians at the landings, hearing of the Black Robe's death, wailed and covered their heads with dust.

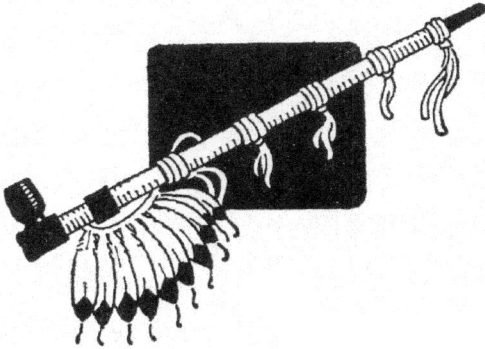

www.ingramcontent.com/pod-product-compliance
Lightning Source LLC
LaVergne TN
LVHW021514080426
835509LV00018B/2505